Journey to France and Spain

1801

VICTOR MARIE DU PONT

From an oil portrait, painted in New York in 1806
by Joseph Bourgoin. The original is now owned by
Mrs. Alfred E. Bissell of Wilmington, Delaware.

JOURNEY TO FRANCE AND SPAIN
1801

BY

Victor Marie du Pont

Edited by Charles W. David, Director,
Eleutherian Mills Historical Library

KENNIKAT PRESS
Port Washington, N. Y./London

JOURNEY TO FRANCE AND SPAIN 1801

Copyright 1961 by Eleutherian Mills—Hagley Foundation
Reissued in 1972 by Kennikat Press
by arrangement with Cornell University Press
Library of Congress Catalog Card No: 70-153259
ISBN 0-8046-1565-9

Manufactured by Taylor Publishing Company   Dallas, Texas

ACKNOWLEDGMENTS

THE preparation of this small volume for publication has involved the labor of many people, whose generous assistance and sympathetic understanding are here gratefully acknowledged. Most important among them have been members, and one former member, of the staff of the Eleutherian Mills Historical Library (formerly the Longwood Library), notably Dr. John B. Riggs, wise scholar and constructive critic, and his assistant, Mrs. Charles J. Aydelotte, Jr.; Mr. Earle E. Coleman, accomplished bibliographer; Miss Grace Ottey, resourceful supplier of books at need; Mrs. Marie Windell, reference and research assistant, and her predecessor, Mrs. David N. Low. It was Mrs. Low who first began work on this project several years ago. Mrs. Windell continued with it and has been tireless in her efforts during the final stages of editing and in seeing the manuscript through press. But the assistant to whom the work owes most has been Mr. Victor de Avenell. Versatile linguist, omnivorous reader, skilled draftsman, and man of many foreign connections, he co-operated with Mrs. Low in the beginning, and he has continued his labors with imaginative resourcefulness to the end. Mr. Ernest F. Saunders, our photographer, has given unfailing co-operation, and Miss Helen E. Lynch, the Director's secretary, has displayed infinite patience in the typing and retyping of manuscripts. It will be perceived that the editor had the good fortune to be the leader of a team.

Outside our immediate circle, help has come from many

Acknowledgments

quarters—in this country, from the Union Library Catalogue of the Philadelphia Metropolitan Area, the University of Pennsylvania Library (especially its Reference Department), and the Library Company of Philadelphia; from the National Archives, the Department of State, and the Library of Congress; from the Maryland Historical Society, from Mr. Charles E. Fenwick, President of the St. Mary's County Historical Society, Leonardtown, Md., and Dr. Wilson Heflin of the United States Naval Academy at Annapolis; from the New York Public Library, the New-York Historical Society, and the Collector of Customs of the Port of New York; from the New England Historic Genealogical Society and from Dr. Benjamin R. Tilden, of Marion, Mass.: abroad, from General Louis de Vaubicourt and Messieurs Jean Denizet and Abel Doysié, all of Paris, and from the Musée Carnavalet of Paris; from the Mayor and from the Municipal Archives of Le Havre; from the Departmental Archives of the Gironde and the Municipal Archives of Bordeaux; from the Chambers of Commerce of Bordeaux and Rochefort and from Monsieur L. Jamet of La Réole; from the Museo Municipal of Madrid and from the United States Consul at Bilbao; from the Historical Service of the French Ministry of War; and from the Library of the British Admiralty in London.

Thanks are also due to Monsieur Jacques-Edmond Bidermann, of Paris, and to Mrs. Alfred E. Bissell and Mrs. Caspar Gordon Sharpless, both of Wilmington, Delaware, for permission to reproduce the ancestral portraits of which they are the owners. The approval of the Board of Trustees of the Longwood Foundation for this edition of Victor du Pont's journal is acknowledged with much gratitude.

It will of course be understood that any errors which may have been made are the sole responsibility of the editor.

CHARLES W. DAVID

Longwood
25 April 1961

CONTENTS

ILLUSTRATIONS

INTRODUCTION

AS the turbulent final decade of the eighteenth century drew to its close, Victor du Pont, then in his early thirties, the elder son of the French economist, Pierre Samuel du Pont de Nemours, seemed well launched on a successful diplomatic career—or so it might have been had not the convulsive upheavals of the French Revolution shattered all normal expectations and rendered any official career precarious. Physically Victor du Pont was splendid, a tall, handsome man with an address that many courtiers might envy. Though his education had not been remarkable, he had inherited from his distinguished father, and had developed through an extended social experience, a capacity to express himself with all the grace that one associates with the ancien régime. These assets were complemented most happily by the woman whom he married in 1794. Josephine du Pont[1] was the youngest daughter of the Marquis de Pelleport and a person of marked perception and savoir-faire. Although she possessed no fortune, an upbringing at Versailles had produced qualities of greater value. Her generous nature and noble character displayed themselves in her devotion to husband and family and to her many friends. Her ability to draw people to her made

---

[1]Gabrielle Joséphine de la Fite de Pelleport (1770–1837), daughter of the Marquis de Pelleport (1724–1783), who was attached to the service of the Comte d'Artois, youngest brother of Louis XVI.

Introduction

her home a popular one. No young diplomat could have asked for a greater asset.

Beginning in 1787, at the age of twenty, Victor du Pont had served three French ministers in the United States: the Comte de Moustier, the Chevalier de Ternant, and Pierre Auguste Adet. Under Adet, who brought him to Philadelphia in 1795, he served as first secretary of the legation, but only briefly. A situation had arisen at Charleston, South Carolina, which called for an immediate replacement of the consul there, and to this important post du Pont had promptly been promoted. He had served successfully in Charleston for more than two years and had then received appointment as consul general in the United States, with orders to proceed to Philadelphia. In all, he had spent six or seven years in the United States, had learned English, and had made a multitude of friends. By now, 1798, he was an experienced official, and it was most unfortunate that relations between France and the United States had deteriorated almost to a state of war. President Adams refused to issue the necessary exequatur for the Philadelphia post, and this denial brought Victor du Pont's diplomatic career to an abrupt end. He felt that there was no choice but to return to France.

Meanwhile the course of events at home had produced a situation that was to turn his life into a completely new channel. Though the government of the incompetent Directory was floundering toward its downfall, Napoleon Bonaparte, who was to bring a new era of hope and confidence, was still confined in Egypt by the power of the British Navy. Political and financial chaos reigned in France. During the intervals when Victor du Pont had been in France, 1790–1791 and 1793–1794, he had played but a minor role in the French Revolution. Not so his father, who had long been active in public life. Du Pont de Nemours had been a prominent member of the States General and the

Introduction

National Constituent Assembly during the early years of the Revolution and narrowly escaped execution during the Reign of Terror. Under the Directory he emerged as a moderate member of the Council of Ancients, only to be expelled from that body by the coup d'état of Fructidor (4 September 1797). Next day, barely avoiding deportation, he was imprisoned in La Force—his second incarceration in that dreaded Paris prison. His younger son, Eleuthère Irénée, was jailed with him, and their printing establishment, which was their principal source of income, was ransacked and some of the presses were broken. Through the influence of friends they were soon released from prison, but du Pont de Nemours was then placed under surveillance at his country estate. Disillusionment with life in France was now complete, and the great family decision was made to emigrate to the United States, where they would establish a new home and seek their fortune.

With characteristic imagination and optimism du Pont de Nemours promptly embarked upon a vast scheme of promotion which, mainly through speculation in American lands, was designed to win great wealth—in which other investors were to be permitted to share. A company to be known as Du Pont de Nemours, Père et Fils & Cie was to be formed with a capital of from 200 to 400 shares, which were to be subscribed at 10,000 francs per share. The purpose of the venture was *"chiefly* to buy and sell land" on the American frontier, but "incidentally to organize any commercial or industrial establishments that may contribute to the improvement of the estates and increase their value." The company was to be directed by Citizen du Pont de Nemours. Its principal leaders were to be a distinguished engineer, Bureaux de Pusy,[2] and the two du Pont brothers, Victor and Irénée.

---

[2]Jean Xavier Bureaux de Pusy, son-in-law of the second Mme du Pont de Nemours (see p. 29 n. 74).

Introduction

Such was the situation which confronted Victor du Pont when he arrived in France with his wife and children in July 1798. By then, plans for the great family venture were far advanced. Apparently his brother had agreed to the project with some enthusiasm. Victor, however, foresaw many difficulties and was reluctant, but his father had made commitments for him. His filial respect was strong, and he accepted, dutifully, the place assigned him. He did his utmost to promote the company and helped in the final preparations for the family's departure for America.

In spite of great efforts the plan to create a large capital through the sale of stock met with only limited success. By 1799 it could be claimed that 241,347 francs had been raised in cash, plus an assignment of 56,000 acres of Kentucky land, valued at one piaster (or Spanish dollar) an acre—far, indeed, from the minimum of two million francs they had set as the original goal. Nevertheless, du Pont de Nemours remained unshaken; with unabated optimism he pressed forward. In May 1799 Bureaux de Pusy and Mme du Pont de Nemours were sent from Rotterdam to New York as a kind of advance guard to establish initial contacts, and in the following October du Pont de Nemours, his two sons, and their families and other relations sailed from the Ile de Ré. After a long and uncomfortable voyage they landed at Newport, Rhode Island, on 3 January 1800.

There were at that time grave difficulties in land speculation throughout America. The fever which had gripped so many European and American investors for years past had driven prices to inflated and highly dangerous levels. Du Pont de Nemours recognized the hazards, and Thomas Jefferson, whose advice he sought, warned him in emphatic terms against investment in anything without the most careful scrutiny. Moreover, the capital which the company had been able to raise was quite inadequate to support extensive speculation in undeveloped lands. Obviously it was necessary to turn in other directions.

Introduction

For this the fertile mind of du Pont de Nemours was ready. Though the firm was not meeting expenses and its meager capital was gradually being consumed, he devised seven distinct schemes, through any one, or several, of which the anticipated fortune might still be won. Each was elaborated in a separate prospectus. Several of the projects would involve the company in serving the French government. If war between France and Britain continued, he reasoned, the company, established in New York, could provide better facilities than the French government itself for marketing sugar from Guadeloupe and French Guiana. If peace followed, the French Navy and French rule in Santo Domingo would have to be re-established. For the Navy a large part of what was needed could be had in the United States; and if the French authorities could be persuaded to use red cedar and white oak in repairs and construction, the resources coming from America would be even greater. All necessary supplies for Santo Domingo were also available in the United States. In all this interchange the company might provide invaluable services to the government—for a commission, of course, which would run to nine or ten million francs a year, and might possibly even rise to eighteen millions. Another scheme involving government patronage proposed the operation of a regular line of packet boats between New York and France. Still another, which was not clearly spelled out, suggested that the French government meet its financial obligations in America by sending merchandise to the United States, where it would be marketed by the company. A further proposal called for a French loan to the United States; this would pass through the company, increase its prestige and credit, and yield a fair commission.

Most ambitious and speculative of all these schemes was one involving a service to Spain in the event that war should continue. Spain was then a French ally, and the threat of British sea power lay between her and a vast overseas empire.

This scheme was not clearly explained because its success would require great secrecy, but du Pont de Nemours estimated it should yield the company five to ten million francs. Finally, with the co-operation of his son Irénée, du Pont de Nemours developed an eighth prospectus, proposing the establishment of a manufactory of gunpowder in the United States with a fairly modest capital of $36,000.

All these ambitious proposals required money, and much more of it than the du Ponts had so far been able to raise. Furthermore, they required promotion not only in France but also in Spain and in the Low Countries. For such activity Victor du Pont was deemed to be particularly well qualified; indeed, his return to Europe in the company's interest had been in contemplation even before the arrival of the family in the United States. Accordingly, du Pont de Nemours discussed the proposals in a long letter to his friend and confidant, Jacques Bidermann, a noted Paris banker. With this letter in their hands, he sent his sons back to France early in 1801.[3]

Irénée du Pont was to develop the powder-manufacturing plan. He was to return to Essonnes, near Paris, the seat of the government's powder manufactory, where he had first studied the art of powder making under the great French chemist Lavoisier. There he was to observe the latest developments and arrange for the acquisition of the most improved machinery. He was also to recruit skilled workmen to operate his mills, once he was ready to commence production.

------

[3]Mme Victor du Pont, writing from New York to her friend Mrs. Gabriel Manigault, of Charleston, S.C., in February 1800, refers to the proposed return of her husband to Europe as a business necessity, and she says, "Le plan en étoit arrêté dès avant notre arrivée" (Mme V. du P. to Mrs. Manigault, 22 Feb. 1800, The Henry Francis du Pont Winterthur Collection of Manuscripts—hereafter cited as Winterthur MSS).

On Bidermann, see below, p. 24, n. 47, and pp. 34, 36, 39, 53, 61.

Introduction

Victor du Pont, the family diplomat, was to devote his energies to a more general promotion of the various plans. Above all, he was to raise additional capital and gain support for all the projects which his father had conceived. He was to seek out investors, both those who had made promises in behalf of the du Pont enterprises before the family left France but had not paid and also potential new subscribers who were still to be won. The acquisition of additional funds was imperative.

He was also to promote with the French government, and notably in naval circles, the several projects which depended upon official support. This was to be done not only by direct recourse to high officials like Consul Lebrun and Forfait, the Minister of Marine, but also among lesser figures who served under the Minister. And there were others, too, among influential men and women, including Mme Bonaparte and the mysterious Mrs. Tilden who "stood pretty well at court and with the ministers through her relationship with Mde Bonaparte."[4] He was to visit Spain also in the interest of the more nebulous project of assisting Spaniards in getting their resources out of South America and the Caribbean despite British domination of the sea. And he was even to undertake to engage in trade on behalf of the company, to earn profits and commissions. Though Victor du Pont was more than eager to return to his family and to the company headquarters in New York, where he felt his restraining influence was needed to curb parental ardor, he persisted in his promotional labors without remission until he sailed from Bordeaux in December 1801.

In spite of these great efforts, it must be acknowledged that his mission was largely a failure. Letters to the company and to his wife carried repeated expressions of discouragement. Little fresh capital was forthcoming for ventures overseas, and his negotiations with French officials were

---

[4]She was formerly Mme Tully, of Martinique (see p. 36, n. 110).

Introduction

unsuccessful. The difficult journey into Spain appears to have achieved nothing, and the Preliminaries of London, which ushered in the end of the naval war, were signed on 1 October[5] before he started for America. Even his minor adventures in trade achieved small success.

A cursory reading of this *Journey to France and Spain*, with its engaging descriptive passages, its record of a pleasant dinner almost every evening, and its frequent references to balls, plays, and the opera, could easily give the impression of a dilettante more addicted to enjoying himself than to the successful conclusion of his mission. Such a judgment, however, would be unfair. A more careful reading of the journal and his letters, especially his business letters, will reveal a serious, hard-working negotiator who did his utmost to succeed, yet one who viewed his father's grandiose dreams with an informed and conscious realism quite unknown in the New York office.

During a period of about ten months Victor du Pont conferred with over two hundred people, some of whom he managed to see repeatedly. Of this number it can be said without hesitation that a good three-quarters involved contacts of a business nature or those which, while seemingly social, were fraught with a business interest. The failures were due to the nature of the promotion he had attempted and to the unfavorable moment when he was required to undertake it, rather than to any want of application and skill. Exactly one week after the du Ponts had set sail for America (2 Oct. 1799), Bonaparte, escaping from Egypt, made a safe landing in the south of France. They were still at sea when one month later the successful coup d'état of 18 Brumaire (9 Nov. 1799) extinguished the weak and divided Directory and raised Bonaparte to virtually supreme power. By the time the du Pont brothers arrived back in Paris in 1801,

---

[5]Followed by the Peace of Amiens (25 March 1802) concluded between France, Spain, and the Batavian Republic on the one hand and Great Britain on the other.

peace had been imposed on most of France's enemies, and before Victor du Pont started for home, it had been all but concluded with her most determined enemy, Great Britain. The establishment of order at home was almost equally dramatic. Thus France in the early years of the Consulate was a land of growing stability and confidence. The tide of emigration had been turned. Investors were becoming more interested in finding profitable uses for their funds in France. They were not disposed to risk them in untried channels such as those which were offered by the firm of Du Pont de Nemours, Père et Fils & Cie.[6]

The autograph manuscript of Victor du Pont's *Journey to France and Spain, 1801* and other documents used in preparing this edition form part of The Henry Francis du Pont Collection of Winterthur Manuscripts, now in the Eleutherian Mills Historical Library, at Greenville, Delaware. The provenance of this collection is somewhat involved. Victor du Pont's papers remained at Louviers, his residence near Wilmington, Delaware, for many years after he died in 1827. The Louviers mansion was later the home of his elder son, Charles Irénée du Pont, who died in 1869. By that date several granddaughters of du Pont de Nemours

[6]The later business career of Victor du Pont was hardly more successful than the initial effort which has here been reviewed. The new trading firm, V. du Pont de Nemours & Co., of New York, which he formed in 1802 upon his father's return to France, succeeded for a time but failed in 1805, largely because the French government refused to honor Santo Domingo drafts on the paymaster of the Navy. His participation in a land development project in 1806 at Angelica, Genesee County, N.Y., was also unsuccessful. Joining his brother, Irénée, on the Brandywine, near Wilmington, Del., in 1809, he undertook the active management of a woolen mill, but here again without notable success. In 1826 he received important recognition as a director of the Second Bank of the U.S. His gifts in politics were greater than in business. He represented New Castle County in the Delaware legislature from 1815 to 1817 and served in the state senate from 1820 to 1822. He died of a heart attack in 1827.

had made great progress in gathering together the family papers. Many of them were arranged and transcribed during this period. Among those who were most active in this work was Sophie Madeleine du Pont, widow of Rear-Admiral Samuel Francis du Pont. Her husband was the younger son of Victor du Pont, and she was the latter's niece. It is known that many of her uncle's papers had passed into her possession by the time she died in 1888. Under the terms of her will all of these family papers passed to her nephew, the late Colonel Henry Algernon du Pont. They were preserved by Colonel du Pont at Winterthur, near Montchanin, Delaware, and willed to his son, Mr. Henry Francis du Pont, through whose generosity and friendly interest the Longwood Foundation, Inc., received full title to the collection in 1959. They have since become part of the resources of the Eleutherian Mills Historical Library.

Inasmuch as this book is the first publication of an edited manuscript to come from the Library, it is necessary to describe in some detail the documents which have been used. The manuscript of the *Journey to France and Spain, 1801* has fortunately survived in Victor du Pont's own hand, in a paper-bound volume of seventy-two leaves (4½ by 7 inches), stitched in six gatherings of twelve. These sheets are of good quality laid paper and bear the watermark of Jan van der Ley, of Zaandyk, Holland. The *Journey* occupies the first sixty-four pages; the remaining ones are blank.

Notwithstanding the interrogation, "How can I employ better the leisure hours of a long passage...?" in the dedication to his wife at the beginning of the journal, one is entitled to doubt that this is Victor du Pont's original record produced from day to day while on his travels. As the facsimile opposite page 28 indicates, this is almost certainly a fair copy, carefully written, and with emendations by the author. It gives the impression of fairly well finished work as far as it goes, but actually it is incomplete. When it breaks off abruptly, practically in the middle of a sentence, with the author's entry into Madrid on 11 May, one can hardly resist the conjecture that he intended to return to his task and complete the narrative.

Within the manuscript itself there is occasional direct evidence of copying. For example, in the entry for 17 February the words "Diamonds are much the fashion now," constituting almost a whole line, are thrust into the middle of a sentence where they do not belong and then deleted. Seven lines farther on they reappear in their proper context. There is also internal evidence that the composition of the manuscript took place long enough after the events described for the author's memory to have dimmed in some degree. For example, in his list of fellow passengers aboard the *Benjamin Franklin* as it sailed from New York he uses the word *Duschéne* as if it were the name of a person, though an examination of the record in the strictly contemporary *Pocket Remembrancer,* discussed below, makes it clear that this word was part of the firm name of Barthélemy, Duchesne & Cie, of Paris.[7] Or, to cite another case, he interrupts his account of the passengers to say, "There was another mess in the steerage," and then continues his listing. This record of a second mess in the steerage seems out of place here, but the parallel passage in the *Pocket Remembrancer,* "Quelques passagers marquan[t]s parmi ceux de l'entrepont," followed by a list of passengers, makes good sense and seems to offer the correct version.[8]

Yet the author did bring home a readable journal of at least a part of his trip. In a letter to her intimate friend Mrs. Gabriel Manigault of Charleston, South Carolina, written on 14 April 1802 only a few weeks after her husband's return, Mme Victor du Pont refers to "un petit journal de la moitié de son voyage, vraiment charmant" which he had brought back to her.[9] One may doubt, however, that this

---

[7]See p. 8 and n. 23.   [8]See p. 9 and n. 29.
[9]Mme V. du P. to Mrs. Gabriel Manigault, 14 April 1802 (Winterthur MSS).

Introduction

was the fair copy of the narrative which has been described above: it is possible that a somewhat earlier version once existed which has since disappeared. The conclusion still seems warranted, therefore, that for Victor du Pont's journey from New York as far as Madrid we have a good, though not exactly contemporary or wholly dependable, manuscript just as it came from the author's hands. This has been made the basis of our text,[10] but it has been carefully checked against the surely contemporary document represented by his notes in *The Gentleman's Annual Pocket Remembrancer for the Year 1801.*[11]

The *Pocket Remembrancer* is a small (2¾ by 4⅝ inches), dilapidated, leather-bound volume of 172 pages. It contains, besides preliminary printed matter, an almanac into which eight blank sheets "for memorandums" are interleaved. This section is followed by a longer one made up of leaves the versos of which consist of "ruled pages [with each line dated] for memorandums, observations, and engagements . . . for every day in the year" and the rectos of vertically ruled pages "for accounts of monies paid, received or lent." In these two sections of nearly ninety pages, arranged in chronological order, Victor du Pont made what appear to be daily notes, though some pages are unused. The remainder of the volume is filled with a variety of printed information of the sort often found in such publications.

This little volume, originally held shut with a strap that has been torn away and lost, has every appearance of having been carried by Victor du Pont on his person during the entire trip and of having been used for daily entries, set down as an aid to memory and perhaps with the deliberate intention of later use in composing a more finished journal.

[10]Excerpts from this manuscript have previously been printed without editing and in a very limited issue in B. G. du Pont, *Lives of Victor and Josephine du Pont* (Newark, Del., 1930).

[11]Printed in Philadelphia by John Bioren for Wm. Y. Birch, 17 South Second St.

Introduction

These notes are for the most part in English. It is reasonable to regard them as the primary material out of which the *Journey to France and Spain, 1801* was developed. As such they merit a more detailed description.

First of all there is a drinking song of five stanzas in French, which appears on both sides of the leaf preceding the almanac page for January. At the end of the last verse the following note is added: "Dicté et parfaitement chanté à bord du parlementaire Benjamin Franklin le 19 janv[ie]r par le C[itoye]n Joseph F. E. Benjamin Anselme Ba[p]tiste, Cap[itain]e au Corps d'Artillerie"—Baptiste being the officer in charge of the prisoners who were being returned to France on that vessel.[12] This is followed by a chronological list of letters written by Victor du Pont to America, with dates, names of addressees, and an indication of the routes by which they were sent. This list appears on both sides of the blank leaf between February and March. It is a satisfaction to observe, at this point, that most of the listed letters are extant today in the Eleutherian Mills Historical Library.

The recto of the next blank leaf, facing April, contains a few memoranda on firms and individuals, the significance of which is not entirely clear. On the next recto, facing June, there is a poem of three stanzas, in French, by Victor du Pont, entitled "Mes Adieux à l'Europe"; at the end he noted, "Wrote the 29th of May, travelling on a mule from Orduña to Bilbao." Then on both sides of the blank leaf between October and November appears a poem, or sea song, of four English stanzas called "The Heaving of the Lead,"[13] and beside it is a somewhat shorter parody of these verses which may well be by Victor du Pont himself. The next blank leaf, opposite the month of December, contains a list of places through which he passed on the journey from San Sebastián to Madrid, Aranjuez, Bilbao, and back again to San Sebas-

---

[12]See p. 9, n. 25.

[13]A somewhat corrupt version of "The Leadman's Song" by Charles Dibdin (1745–1814).

tián, with distances carefully given in Spanish leagues and occasional brief notes on the countryside through which he passed.

The versos of the next and longer section of the *Pocket Remembrancer* are filled with memoranda of events, beginning with Monday, 5 January, when he wrote, "Parti de New York sur le Benjamin Franklin à 3 h[eures] après midi." The rectos are used, first, for a list of fellow passengers and, then, for a record of the author's winnings and losses, mostly the latter, in various card games of the day—*brelan,* cribbage, reversi, *bouillotte,* faro, and twenty-one. Not all recto pages are so used, however, for there are occasional descriptive passages about a city, the countryside, roads, or buildings, notably during the trip to Spain; and, finally, since he did not return to New York until early February 1802, he turned backward at the end of December and used the last rectos for daily comments on the final stages of his homeward voyage. Thus we have in the brief entries of this little volume dated memoranda for his entire trip.

But these brief, sometimes cryptic, notes in the *Pocket Remembrancer* do not constitute all of the traveler's original record. A small blank notebook entitled, "Journey to France, 1801, Day Book, Expences," offers additional evidence. This is a pocket-sized volume (3⅞ by 6⅜ inches) of 44 leaves stitched in a single gathering with a cover of heavy marbled paper. Ink-stained, worn, and soiled, it presents every appearance of having had constant use. Apparently it was Victor du Pont's intention to record in it all his expenses, business and personal, presumably to facilitate reimbursement of the former by the company. This is strictly an expense account, without notes or comments on events, but because of its exact chronology, the record of places where expenses were incurred, and the nature of some of the expenses recorded, e.g., "Guns for Irénée, Bauduit, and Orsel," "Mounting an engraving for Mde Bonap[arte]," "Books and Caricatures," "Pins and garters for Josephine," it does supply much exact

Introduction

supplementary information which is often of interest and sometimes helpful in interpreting the journal itself.

This comprehensive expense account is not all that has survived of Victor du Pont's financial record. Another less worn, more attractive, carefully written notebook entitled, "Journey to Europe in acc[oun]t with the Company, 1801," is also extant. This volume (4¾ by 7 inches) contains twenty leaves stitched in a single gathering, with covers of heavy marbled paper. It appears to be a fair copy of business, or company, expenses posted, for the most part, from the original "Day Book, Expences" and prepared with a view to reimbursement. It will be referred to hereafter as the "Company Expense Account."

Still a third account book survives. It is a volume (4½ by 7 inches) stitched in a single gathering, without cover or title. This contains summations of expenses, arranged chronologically under such headings as "Cloathing, Dressing, etc.," "Villars' Account" (i.e., the account of outlays for a personal servant of that name), "Various Expences in France, needful, incidental, and unavoidable," "Pleasure Expences, Comedy, Balls, Parties, Cards, etc." This booklet is referred to hereafter as the "Classified Expense Account." All three of these account books are filled with exact data which can be drawn upon, from time to time, to confirm or supplement the meager entries of the *Pocket Remembrancer*. There is, indeed, a fourth account book marked "Ledger" (4½ by 7⅛ inches), of twenty-eight leaves stitched in a single gathering, covered in leather. This is arranged as a double-entry account, but it has proved extremely difficult to interpret and may well be incomplete. Very little use has been made of it.

Finally it should be remarked that most of the letters between Victor du Pont and his wife during this period have survived; only three of the twenty he wrote are missing. Besides these he wrote a considerable number to the firm in New York and to other business connections. Some have survived as sent, and all have survived in summary form, at least, in a manuscript entitled "Correspondance de Victor du Pont quand il était en Europe, 1801";[14] this will be referred to hereafter as "Letter Book—1801." This correspondence offers information of much interest in an elucidation of the journal. From the foregoing it is apparent that the *Journey to France and Spain, 1801* is extremely well documented.

In the editing of the manuscript of the *Journey to France and Spain, 1801* for publication, a middle course has been followed, with insistence upon neither exact textual reproduction nor complete modernization. It must be noted, however, that Victor du Pont was a Frenchman and that his knowledge of English could not be expected to equal that of an Englishman or an American. Largely for this reason it has been necessary to make certain corrections in order to produce a clear, smooth narrative.

As a rule the author's errors of spelling and grammar have been allowed to stand, the only exceptions being those cases where changes were required to present a more readable text. As a foreigner who had learned English after reaching maturity, Victor du Pont had continual difficulty with certain small words like *than, that,* and *as.* Nor had he fully mastered the singular and plural forms of certain verbs. In such cases corrections have been made in the text and the manuscript readings given in footnotes. The author was sometimes uncertain, too, about the use of single and double letters; here missing letters have usually been supplied between brackets. Where it was necessary to delete a letter, the original form has been placed in a footnote. Many misspellings arise from the author's familiarity with the French form of a word which is common to the two languages but is spelled differently in English. Such gallicisms seem harmless

[14]This manuscript is divided between two collections in the Eleutherian Mills Historical Library, the Winterthur MSS and the Longwood Manuscripts, the latter hereafter cited as Longwood MSS.

Introduction

and can lead to no misunderstanding. They have, therefore, been left unchanged.

The author's use of underscoring in the manuscript is inconsistent. Sometimes he underlined such a foreign, or mixed, phrase as *ancient régime,* or a personal name, or the title of a play or an opera; sometimes he did not. Here it has seemed best to indicate such underscoring, by means of italics, when there appeared to be a justifiable reason for it; otherwise it has been ignored, and italics have not been supplied in some cases where good modern usage would require them.

The author sometimes employed initial capitals in common nouns or adjectives, perhaps for emphasis, an eighteenth-century practice which modern usage rejects. In most such cases his form has been preserved. On the other hand, he often omitted capitals where they are required today. This was notably true at the beginning of sentences and of proper names. Here capital letters have been supplied as needed, without notation.

Problems of punctuation have been most difficult of all. The author's favorite mark was a dash, which can signify a full stop, a comma, or a semicolon. Yet he did use periods, commas, and semicolons, though very often he omitted punctuation altogether. To produce a good, readable text, with his punctuation alone, seemed impracticable. A number of compromises have, therefore, been resorted to, though they have been introduced sparingly. Admittedly this action calls for a degree of faith in editorial judgment and ability not to distort the author's meaning.

The spelling of proper names has presented peculiar difficulties. Here also the practice has been to give a corrected spelling in the text and to place the manuscript reading in a footnote. Occasional exceptions have been made, as, for example, letting such a place name as Port Passage stand in the text rather than replacing it with Pasajes (near San Sebastián).

Contractions and abbreviations have, with few exceptions,

been expanded by placing the supplied portions within brackets. Superscribed letters have regularly been lowered to the line. The word *and* has been supplied in the place of the ampersand, which the author uses often but not consistently. For the symbol &ᵃ *(et cetera)*, the modern form, *etc.*, has been substituted. The feminine title Madame, which the author commonly contracts to Mde, instead of the modern Mme, has been left unchanged.

The *Journey to France and Spain, 1801* contains the names of many people. Much of the work of editing the journal for publication has, therefore, involved their identification. This has not always been easy or successful; a few names still elude the editor. Where information has been derived from well-known published works of reference, specific citation has been omitted in the documentation; but when it has come from less obvious sources, or from manuscripts, references have been given.

The identification of place names has not been a serious problem. What seemed more immediate for a clear appreciation of the text is the geographical location of the places mentioned. For places outside France and Spain footnotes have been used, but for the many places which Victor du Pont visited in both these countries, it seemed simpler to indicate them on a map (p. 67). All such places are listed in the index.

C. W. D.

Journey to France and Spain

1801

GABRIELLE JOSEPHINE (DE LA FITE DE PELLEPORT) DU PONT
From an early oil portrait by an unknown artist. The original is now
owned by Mrs. Caspar Gordon Sharpless of Wilmington, Delaware.

To Josephina d[u] P[ont]   V[ictor] d[u] P[ont]

Of earthly goods the best is a good wife!

J'ai trouvé en elle Esprit, sagesse, beauté, graces, délicatesse de sentiments, noblesse dans les manières, grandeur d'âme, douceur de caractère—en un mot tout ce qu'on ne peut désirer d'un même objet sans témérité.
> —*Lettres de la C[omte]sse de la Rivière*[1]

To you my good Friend I dedicate this journal, it is for you I write it. How can I employ better the leisure hours of a long[2] passage which appears to me the most tedious I ever made, such is my impatience to embrace you and my dear Children.

---

[1] *Lettres de Madame la comtesse de la Rivière, à Madame la baronne de Neufpont, son amie* (Paris, 1777), II, 220. Victor du Pont's copy of vol. II (edition of 1776) of this work is in the Eleutherian Mills Historical Library.

[2] In the MS the word *tedious* has been struck out before *long*.

JANUARY 1801

The Business of our new establish'd house[3] in New York requiring that one of us should go to Paris and stay there some time, the lot fell on me; and it was determined in the end of December that I should take passage on the Benjamin Franklin, one of my friend Breuil's vessels,[4] which was coming from Philadelphia in order to take some French prisoners to Havre de Grace[5] with pas[s]-ports from the British Consul.[6]

---

[3]Du Pont de Nemours, Père et Fils & Cie.

[4]Francis Breuil, 115 Spruce St., Philadelphia, a merchant and ship-owner with whom the du Ponts long had important business relations. He not only owned the *Benjamin Franklin* but also the *Missouri,* the *Eugénie,* the *Neptune,* and probably other vessels. As late as Nov. 1812 E. I. du Pont was urging his father to come back to America by one of the vessels which Breuil was sending to France (*Life of Eleuthère Irénée du Pont from Contemporary Correspondence,* translated from the French by B. G. du Pont [11 vols. and index; Newark, Del., 1923–1927], hereafter cited as *Life of E. I. du Pont*).

[5]The great French port of Le Havre at the mouth of the Seine.

[6]France and Britain had been continuously at war since 1793. In his *Pocket Remembrancer* Victor du Pont described the *Benjamin Franklin* as a cartel ship *(parlementaire)*. The British consul in question was doubtless Thomas Barclay (1753–1830), who was consul general in New York from 1799 until his death.

My brother Irenée came with me. His object was to get instructions and machines for the erection of powder's mills, and he was to return by the same vessel. We left New York with a fine North West wind Monday the 5th of Jan[uar]y at 3 o'clock in the afternoon.[7]

We were very nigh running ashore on Governors Island[8] reef; the pilot was as pale as death when he saw how close to the rocks the wind kept us. But the danger was soon over.

---

[7]The dollar record from Day Book, Expences, showing Victor's outlays for the trip before leaving New York is of such interest as to require full quotation:

Passage on board the Benjamin Franklin	$ 140.00
Making of Matrasses Covers and Pillars [pillows]	8.00
Cotton for d[itt]o	74.70
Blanket	1.50
A furr Cap	2.50
Woosted stokings	2.00
Provisions for passage	40.00
Box of liquors	12.50
Bottle of bitters	1.25
Spoons knive and plate	1.00
Pair of woosted trowsers	3.00
3 boxes of 500 Segars	20.00
Mackassoons [Mocassins]	1.25
Books Almanacks etc.	3.00
Boat and Cart for trunks	1.25
Thread etc.	.50
Segars American	1.00
Woosted Gloves	.50
Pocket Book	2.50
Tumblers etc.	.50
	$316.95

In the margin of this account Victor records the sale, after his arrival at Le Havre, of the cotton in his bedding for 512 livres, a transaction on which he figured he had made a profit of 120 livres. He was evidently using a conversion rate of 5.25 livres to the dollar.

[8]MS *Governor island's.*

It was the second passage I [had] made on the Benjamin Franklin. We came over to Bord[eau]x in her in 1798. She is a fine large vessel of 280 tons copper bottom'd and sailing very fast. The Good and amiable Capt. Lloyd[9] Jones had left her and it was a great loss. Capt. Antho[n]y Senkey who commands her now is a very smart sailor.

Though begin[n]ing our voyage with a fair wind, the first moments were, as they are always, disagreeable enough, especially when there are many passengers; the mind, soured by the affliction of leaving one's friends and family, is little disposed to the calmnes[s], forbearance and tranquillity without which you cannot extricate yourself of the general confusion nor avoid being very much incommoded by those who are sick by nature or assuming by character.

We were 11 sleeping and 15 eating in the Cabin—upon the whole as good a mess as could be expected.[10]

My next neighbour after my brother was Maximilien Joseph de Caumont, who was known in America under the name of *the Little French Count,* and whose appearance did not command even as much regard and respect as this nickname would admit of. However he turned out to be quite another man than I expected—polite, sensible, well-bread, having much improved by his extensive travels, and his conversation being both instructive and agreable. I made a friendship with him.[11]

---

[9]MS *Cape Loid.*

[10]In his first letter to his wife (4 Feb.) upon landing at Le Havre he says: "Les 15 premiers jours nous avons fait mauvaise cuisine parce que la mer était beaucoup trop grosse et les 15 autres parce que les chaudières étaient beaucoup trop petites pour une table de 15 personnes ayant bon appétit" (V. du P. to Mme V. du P., 4 Feb. 1801, Winterthur MSS).

[11]This gentleman had evidently been a subject of discussion between Victor and his wife before the departure from New York. In his first letter to her after his landing he says: "Je te prie de réhabiliter Caumont dans l'opinion de ta société intime; c'est un jeune homme très instruit qui a voyagé dans les 4 coins du monde, qui a bien

Nicholas Warin,[12] born in Amsterdam and educated in England, was a handsome and amiable young man with great deal of *savoir vivre,* a perfection which the French have denominated and which no nations in Europe posess less than they do in general. There is more *savoir vivre* to be found in the lowest class of people in[13] the United States than there was in France in the middle Class before the Revolution and than[14] there is now in the first Class compos'd of Generals and *Fournisseurs.*[15]

To return to our passagers, we had four officers of the ancient regime, emigrants returning under the protection of [the] Bonaparte administration—Coutellier, Felix St. Hilaire, de Gouro, and de Rouer.[16] The first was an officer

---

observé et raconte fort agréablement; il fait des vers, et est de plus aimable et bon compagnon" (V. du P. to Mme V. du P., 4 Feb. 1801, Winterthur MSS). Mme Victor du Pont has, however, left a very damaging account of him. In a letter to her friend Mrs. Manigault, of Charleston, she says: "Le petit comte qui en fesoit tant, est parti avec nos pauvres voyageurs. Il a eu la distraction d'oublier de payer son *boarding.* On a envoyé un constable, mais le vaisseau était au large. Ce dernier fait l'achève comme vous jugez bien ici" (Mme V. du P. to Mrs. Gabriel Manigault, 25 Jan. 1801, Winterthur MSS). In the "Registre d'enregistrement des Passeports 1801 de la Ville du Havre," Archives Municipales du Havre (hereafter cited as the Havre Register of Passports), his name is given as Joseph Combette Caumont.

[12]Presumably Nicolaas Warin (1744–1815). Dismissed from the City Council of Amsterdam with the fall of the stadholderate and the triumph of revolutionary France (1795), he remained out of public office until after Napoleon's downfall. In the last year of his life he became president of the upper chamber of the Dutch legislature and a peer of the realm *(Nieuw Nederlandsch Biografisch Woordenboek,* Leiden, 1911–   ). In the notes in the *Pocket Remembrancer,* opposite the monthly calendar for April, the author gives his address as "Heregrach [i.e., the famous Heeren Gracht] near the Reguliers grach, Amsterdam." Warin is mentioned again, in Paris, p. 59.

[13]A word of several letters has been struck out after *in.*

[14]MS *that.*

[15]Contractors.

[16]In the *Pocket Remembrancer* these four returning émigrés are listed as follows: "LeCoustelier, anc[ie]n off[icie]r du Reg[imen]t du

in the Regiment du Roy, a good honest fellow, *un peu bègue
et passablement ennuyeux*.[17] St. Hilaire had been a midship-
man before the Revolution. He has a sweet countenance and
very soft manners. Gouro looks and smell[s] very much like
a Cherokee Indian and is a great glutton; but these are only
ridicules and do[18] not prevent his being a very worthy
respectable man. Himself and two brothers supported themselves five years in America by cultivating with their own
hands a small farm near Trenton. They had no servant,
ploughed the ground and carried their butter and pigs to
market themselves. They were all officers in the army and
had [had] more than [a] hundred thousand livres revenue
between them.

De Rouer, an old man, had been a petty officer in the
king['s] body guards and went also to America without any
other ressource but the work of his hands. He is a perfect
caricature of the ancient regime, and indeed one would
think he was born 200 years ago by his notions and manners
—not less respectable for being out of fashion now, for the
Age of Chivalry is gone as Mr. Burke says.

Hamon of Wilmington[19] had the mate state room. He has

Roi"; "St. Hilaire, anc[ie]n off[icie]r de Marine"; "de Gouro, ancien
off[icie]r d'Inf[anter]ie"; "de Rouer, ancien off[icie]r des Gardes du
Corps." In the Havre Register of Passports, 1801, they appear as
François Pierre Marie Le Coustellier, Félix St. Hilaire, Louis Constantin Ange Gourreaux, and René Binjamin [sic] Rouër. St. Hilaire
presented a certificate stating that he had been a resident of the
United States since Jan. 1793, and declared his intention of proceeding
to Paris.

[17]A bit of a stammerer and somewhat tiresome.

[18]MS *does*.

[19]William Hamon, of Wilmington (1752–1816), a French businessman who had arrived in this country via Santo Domingo. He became
an intimate associate of E. I. du Pont and represented him in the
purchase of the original Broom property on the Brandywine on which
the powder mill was to be erected. For a time he had a minor share
in the business, but he withdrew in 1803, giving as his reason his
terrible losses in Santo Domingo. In spite of some difficulties, the

a representation and a modest insurance that will every-where claim the head of the table, and we gave it to him with so much more pleasure that he had an abondance of private stores of the best quality.

Castillon of Bordeaux[20] is a young man who had been obliged to fly, being prosecuted on account of his exertions against the Jacobins before the 18 of Fructidor.[21]

Magon of St. Malo[22] is a relation to the Bankers of Paris, was an inhabitant of S[an]t[o] Domingo—and a very discreet, well bred, amiable man.

Tierlin is a clerck of the house of Barthelemy [and] Duschéne of Paris, who was very willing to make us beleive that he was an ambassador extraordinary, or some such thing, and had the fate of France and America in his hands —a complete Parisian coxcomb.[23]

---

friendship and business relations between Hamon and the du Ponts persisted at least as late as 1811. He is said to have died in Philadelphia in 1816 (*Life of E. I. du Pont, passim*).

[20]In the *Pocket Remembrancer* Victor calls him "Henry Castillon de Bordeaux."

[21]The coup d'état of 18 Fructidor (4 Sept. 1797) by which, with Bonaparte's assistance, a faction of the Directory, faced with a strong conservative and royalist reaction, overthrew their opponents in the legislative councils and in the Directory and kept the regicides in power.

[22]In the Havre Register of Passports, 1801, he appears as Auguste Magon. He may have been a member of the well-known Breton family to which belonged Jean Baptiste Magon de Labalue, banker to the royal court, executed in 1794, and also Admiral Charles René Magon, who was killed in the battle of Trafalgar.

[23]The author has fallen into confusion in this sentence—a con-fusion which may indicate that he was writing his finished text some time after his journey had ended and when his memory was growing faint. His text, into which the word *and* has been inserted, is so written as to give the impression that Duschéne was another returning pas-senger. But the pertinent text in the *Pocket Remembrancer* makes it clear that Duschéne was part of the name of a business firm, actually Barthélemy Duchesne & Cie, Paris bankers. It reads, "Tierlin co-m[m]is de Barthé[lem]y & Duschéne." The Havre Register of Passports,

Guilbert[24] is a young fool, half French half Prussian, from Neuchatel—half bear half monkey, if these were not two very sensible animals.

Capt. Ba[p]tiste,[25] officer of artillery from Santo Domingo[26] was the Capt. in chief of our gang of ragamuffins, prisoners, sailors, which he kept in pretty good order, to our great satisfaction; for we had no little apprehension of their rising upon us to take the ship and carry her as a prise to Santo Domingo.[27] He is[28] a brother to the famous Ba[p]tistes, the players of Paris, and has been on the stage himself. He is a handsome agreable man.

There was another mess in the steerage.[29] Some of them

1801, records this passenger as Ch[arl]es Étienne Tierlin and describes him as a "négociant."

[24]Presumably Henri Guillebert, who is described as a "négociant" in the Havre Register of Passports, 1801. Other information about him is lacking.

[25]Joseph François Eugène Benjamin, Baron Anselme, called Baptiste (1772–1810), member of a family of actors at the Théâtre Français, who rose through a military career to the rank of an officer of the Legion of Honor and a baron of the Empire. In 1801 he held the rank of captain and was being returned home from Santo Domingo on grounds of health (see the article on him in the *Dictionnaire de biographie française*, ed. J. Balteau, M. Barroux, and M. Prévost [Paris, 1933–   ] under "Anselme"; see also V. du P. to Talleyrand, Le Havre, 15 Pluviose An IX [4 Feb. 1801], Archives des Affaires Étrangères [France], Correspondance Politique, États-Unis, vol. LIII, no. 4).

[26]MS *St. Domingue.*

[27]MS *St. Domingue.*

[28]MS *his.*

[29]Here again the author may have fallen into confusion, perhaps due to a fading memory. It is difficult to see why he should refer to a second mess in the steerage and then proceed to comment on five additional passengers. His much briefer entry in the *Pocket Remembrancer* seems to make better sense. It is as follows:

Quelques passagers marquan[t]s parmi ceux de l'entrepont:

LeLieur

Koenig Botaniste

we have not seen once in the passage and others [a] great deal too much. Mr. Dubois,[30] a most enraged Jacobin,[31] was one of this last number.

Our friend and neighbour,[32] Lelieur,[33] slept there and has been sick almost all the passage. Two French ladies with a child have not been out of their bed more than once.

Capt. Viaud of Nantes,[34] a very polite man though a privateer.

Mr. Poulet,[35] surgeon in the Navy, was on board the

Poulet off[icie]r de Santé *des Déportés*
Dubois *Jacobin forcené*
Viau Cap[itai]ne de nav[ir]e de Nantes.

[30]In the Havre Register of Passports, 1801, he is recorded as Citoyen François Dubois, and it is noted that, having left France after the enactment of the law which closed the list of émigrés and bearing a valid passport, he is authorized to proceed to Paris, "lieu de son domicile."

[31]One of the extreme Jacobins during the period of the Terror who were commonly called the *Enragés*.

[32]MS *neighbourg*.

[33]Presumably Jean Baptiste Louis, Comte Lelieur de Ville-sur-Arce (1765–1849), who had been in charge of parks, gardens, and nurseries under the monarchy and was again to hold that position under the Empire. He is said to have introduced the sweet potato *(patate d'Amérique)* into France. He is the author, among other things, of *La pomone française, ou Traité de la culture et de la taille des arbres fruitiers* (Paris, 1817). For his continuing contacts with the du Ponts, particularly with a view to exchanging plants and seeds between France and America, see *Life of E. I. du Pont, passim.* In the Havre Register of Passports, 1801, he appears as Jean Louis Lelieur.

[34]MS *Nantz.* In the Havre Register of Passports, 1801, this privateer, called Ferdinand Viaud, is listed as a seaman *(marin)* who had come from "un bâtiment français qui a été pris par une frégate américaine au mois de floréal an 8" (April-May, 1800).

[35]According to the Havre Register of Passports, 1801, this was "Jacques Lazare Poulet, natif de la commune des Coteaux, Isle de St. Domingue, domicilié à St. Domingue." He declared his intention of proceeding to Paris. He was, however, held at Le Havre, until 22 Feb., when an order was received from the Minister of Marine for him to proceed to Rochefort and present himself to the prefect there. On his

frigate that carried the Deportés of the 18th of Fructidor
to Cayenne.[36]

And Koenig,[37] a Dutch botanist coming over with a great
provision of seeds. [These] are the only one[s] worth
remembering.

I must not forget however Mr. Petit de Villers,[38] supercargo[39] of the ship, whose obliging and friendly behaviour
has been gratefully acknowledged and whom I have considered since as my particular friend.

Nothing particular happen'd till Thursday the 15th when
at 8 o'clock in the evening, a cloudy squally weather, we
plainly saw light fires, which they call in French *feu St.*

---

second appearance before the mayor of Le Havre he is described as
aide-de-camp of General Rigaud.

[36]Cayenne, capital of French Guiana, was the center of the penal
settlements to which were sent a large number of deported persons,
including many deputies, following the coup d'état of 18 Fructidor.
Many of them died there.

[37]Strange as it may seem, this botanist was Mathias Kin, regarding
whom see U. P. Hedrick, *History of Horticulture in America* (New
York, 1950), pp. 400–401, and Townsend Ward, "The Germantown
Road and Its Associations," *Pennsylvania Magazine of History*, VI
(1882), 396–398. Several of his letters are among the Winterthur MSS,
and he regularly signs himself as above. In the Havre Register of Passports, 1801, he is listed as Mathieu Kin. Although Victor calls him
Koenig, his brother, Irénée, consistently refers to him as King, the
English equivalent of Koenig (E. I. du P. to Pichon, 7 Oct. 1801;
E. I. du P. to Joseph de Dreux, 12 Nov. 1801, Winterthur MSS), and
describes him as a German *(allemand)* botanist who was not a savant
but "un jardinier instruit qui connaît la pratique et la langue de la
chose." Kin himself refers to a commission which he had to collect in
this country for the "Collège botanique de Strasbourg" (Mathias Kin
to E. I. du P., 29 Sept. 1801); and E. I. du Pont, calling him King,
refers to this same commission in the letter to Pichon cited above.

[38]Arriving in Paris on 12 Feb. as Victor's traveling companion, he
appears frequently in later pages of the journal. He seems to have
continued as supercargo on the *Benjamin Franklin* and to have been
on the ship on Victor's return voyage from Bordeaux in the following
December.

[39]MS *subercargo*.

Elme,[40] at the end of every yard and on the top of the masts.

The wind had been westerly since our departure, some times very strong with heavy seas. The 17th we went at the rate of 10 knots ½ the whole day.

Monday 19th—for the first time Contrary winds. I met with the severest fall I ever[41] had in my life; it was very slipery on deck and I fell all at once on my forehead with such violence that I saw a thousand lights, was giddy for some moments, and though nothing had touched but the middle of my forehead, I had a black eye.

Till the 22d—we had south winds and calms. The weather very warm and damp creates many colds and fevers on board.[42]

To the 27th—variable winds and pretty good weather. We were visited that day by a French privateer brig, the Grand Decidé de Bordeaux. He has the reputation to be a fast sailor and must really be so, for not having been taken yet; however he was very long a-coming up with us and would not have had us before night had we not[43] shorten[ed] sail. The Captain came himself on board, and was very fond of talking; he staid near two hours and would have staid much longer had not two sails appeared in sight.

The 28th—23 days after our departure we struck bottom at 95 fathoms.[44]

The 29th—80 fathoms of[f] Scilly.[45] At 11 o'Clock in the night we were visited by the British fregate Glenmore, Capt.

---

[40]St. Elmo's fire.

[41]MS *hever*.

[42]On this same date the author records the position in his *Pocket Remembrancer* as follows: "Latitude observ[e]d 47° 26′, first observation for nine days."

[43]Several letters have been struck out after *not*.

[44]The record in the *Pocket Remembrancer* for this date is: "Beautifull weather fine N.W. winds, sounded 95 fathoms."

[45]The Scilly Isles, off Cornwall.

Duff.[46] She kept us more than 3 hours. The Capt. was so drunk that he could not read our passport, and would not understand any thing that was said by our Capt. or his own lieut[e]nants. He sent 3 times to have the hull visited; they found 5 or 6 boxes well packed and he ordered them on board the fregate. They were seeds of American trees belonging to my brother and Lelieur. It would have been a very infortunate circomstance had they been open[ed] for in some of them there were[47] [a] few shawls and muslin pieces for presents to his female friends in Paris. The boxes were already on deck when Capt. Duff[48] fell asleep and his first lieuten[an]t ordered Capt. Senkey to go on board and make sail.

Friday 30th—at 12 o'clock we were visited by the British 74, Canada,[49] Capt. de Courcy.[50] In the night we were spoke to by another man of war. We saw Start Point[51] in the morning of Saturday, spoke a British fregate which asked[52] us who we were and where we were bound, having received signals from the other Cruizers. In the evening we saw Portland Bill[53] and the Isle of Wight[54] lighthouses.

[46]MS *Dough.* George Duff (1764–1805). He had been the captain of the *Glenmore* since 9 April 1796 but was succeeded by John Talbot on 8 Feb. 1801. In 1805 he was commander of the *Mars* in the battle of Trafalgar and lost his life in that famous action. He was a grand-nephew of Vice-Admiral Robert Duff (d. 1787) and father of Vice-Admiral Norwich Duff (d. 1862). See R. H. Mackenzie, *The Trafalgar Roll* (London, 1913), p. 122, n. 1.

[47]MS *was.*   [48]MS *Dough.*

[49]A ship of the Royal Navy, third class, mounting 74 guns.

[50]Hon. Michael de Courcy (d. 1824), third son of the twenty-fifth Baron Kingsale, captain, Royal Navy, 1783, later Admiral of the Blue and Knight of the Tower and Sword.

[51]Start Point is a narrow headland projecting eastward a few miles south of Dartmouth Harbor.

[52]MS *told.*

[53]At the extreme tip (with a lighthouse still) of the rocky peninsula called the Isle of Portland, which extends south from the Dorset coast.

[54]MS *Whight.*

FEBRUARY

Sunday morning—saw Cape Barfleur[1] and intered into Havre[2] harbour. There we found 3 English fregates. One of them, the Loire,[3] kept us a long time and so we lost the tide and the chance to get into port that day, as no pilot durst come on board as long as the English staid with us.

Next day, Monday the 2d of February—we intered Havre[4] de Grace docks at 12 o'clock. The whole town was crowding on the warfs to see us; the Britishs keep so close a blockade on this port that no vessel of size had been here for more than 3 years. It was a great sight for the grand nation of this little place.

A selected party of us collected together in the same tavern, Hotel de la Marine, chez Mde Le Gris—a pretty good house and very good people.

It is but a poor sight, as[5] the prettiest town in Europe, for persons accustomed to live in America; and though Havre[6] is a genteel place in comparison with many other[s], it was [a] few days before I could reconcile myself with the idea of streets narrow and dark, full of mud and rubbish, of houses so dirty in the outsides and never washed in the interior, of people so strangely dressed, especially the women, of their woosted caps and wooden shoes, and above all, of these miserable looking creatures which swarm[7] everywhere, the beggars.

Amongst the many instances of the Superiority of young flourishing America over[8] old decayed France,[9] the regula-

---

[1]At the northeast extremity of the department of Manche, as one enters the Bay of the Seine.

[2]MS *Haver.*

[3]A vessel of 46 guns which had been taken from the French.

[4]MS *Haver.*   [5]MS *than.*

[6]MS *Haver.*   [7]MS *swarms.*   [8]MS *on.*

[9]This attitude of the author is somewhat surprising; he did not become a citizen of the U.S. until July 1802.

tion of Custom houses is one of the most striking for a stranger. There is no equality no justice; it is all vexation or all corruption. There are[10] more custom house officers in one port of France where no trade is carried on, than there are in the whole of the United States. These poor wretches have only from 300 to 500 livres salary a year; and they must starve or steal, and consequently do the last. They will beg for a morsel of bread, receive 12 sols and put in their pocket every thing they can lay hold of.[11] There came more than 20 of them on board of the Franklin and they made a glorious day of it; not one trunk was open[ed] and many of us who had goods, smuggled them with the consent of the officers without any other difficulty than putting one crown in their hands.

Tuesday the 3d—we all went to the municipality for our passports and many of us met with great difficulties. In consequence of the late attempt on the life of Bonaparte on the 3d of Nivose,[12] the minister of police, Fouché,[13] a great Jacobin who wished[14] the people to believe that it was the Royalists who wanted to destroy the Consul and not his friends the anarchists, sent circulars to all the ports against the entrance of emigrants. The municipality is well composed of honest moderate men but very much effrayed of their masters and very much perplexed to draw a proper line between their inclination and their duty. Some were detained till the minister of police should have determined if they could be permitted to go in[to] the interior and some,

---

[10]MS *is.*

[11]MS *off.*

[12]24 Dec. 1800. The reference is to the royalist plot to assassinate Bonaparte. As he was passing through a little side street, the rue Saint-Nicaise, on his way to the Opéra, an "infernal machine" was exploded in his path. More than twenty people were killed, but the First Consul escaped.

[13]Joseph Fouché (1750–1820), a notorious figure of the revolutionary and Napoleonic epoch.

[14]The word *wanted* has been struck out and changed to *wished.*

[15]

who had no better right, were admitted through chance or their own consequence and forwardness.

My passport being as a merchant, they suffered me to go to Paris immediately; but my brother who thought himself more secure still, having a passport as [a] Botanist sent by the National Institute, was very nigh being detained with the emigrants. Merchants were[15] designated as free by the instructions of the minister of police but there was not a word in them respecting botanists; and the wise *municipaux* had agreed unanimously that they should write on that subject and that the poor Botanist should remain as a proof of their caution and devotion to the minister. Irenée did not take the jocke and we went together to expostulate, I[16] proposing gravely to turn a botanist and let him be the merchant, as his time was more precious than mine. However the name of my father being soon introduced, he is so generally beloved and respected that in his consideration the municipality revised their *arrêté* and agreed that[17] a *botanist* might not be a conspirator.

The 4th—I saw in the morning several merch[an]ts: Mr. Faure,[18] the sousprefet,[19] and his father,[20] one of the 73 members of the Convention who protested and were prison-

---

[15]MS *where*.   [16]MS *my*.   [17]MS *than*.

[18]Guillaume Stanislas Faure (1765–1826), second son of Pierre Joseph Denis Guillaume Faure. Born in Le Havre, he was a printer before the Revolution. He was made subprefect of Le Havre in the year VIII (1799–1800) and became a member of the Legislative Body under the Empire. In the 1820's he published two substantial works on nautical geography.

[19]Subprefect.

[20]Pierre Joseph Denis Guillaume Faure (1726–1818). Born in Le Havre, he began his career in the Navy but turned to the law and became a judge in Le Havre in 1791. Elected to the Convention in 1792, he was expelled and imprisoned in 1793 and recalled in 1794 after the fall of Robespierre. Returning to Le Havre after the Convention, he resumed his place as judge. He was ennobled by Louis XVIII in 1815 (A. Kuscinski, *Dictionnaire des conventionnels* [Paris, 1916]).

ers in the Luxembourg.[21] In the evening Henry Homberg[22] carried us to a Concert where we heard pretty good music and saw some handsome ladies.

The 5th—dined with Mr. Gregoire Homberg. A great display of provincial show and mercantile affluence; these Hombergs are the ugliest family I ever saw, but very good people, certainly the richest house in Havre.[23] Their ennemies say[24] they are great Jews, but it may be jealousy altogether.

The 6th—dined with Edward Homberg. This part of the family is the less disgraced by nature. The mother is an English woman. The father has been Dutch Consul in England.

---

[21]The reference is to the 73 (more correctly the 75) members of the Right in the Convention who had signed protests on 6 and 19 June against the violent expulsion on 2 June 1793 of the 22 Girondist deputies. Their arrest was moved by Deputy Amar and voted by the Convention 3 Oct. 1793. Their surviving remnants were recalled to the Convention after the fall of Robespierre 27 June 1794 (9 Thermidor An ıı).

[22]The Hombergs before the Revolution had been one of the great commercial houses of Le Havre, and in spite of great losses in Santo Domingo due to the insurrection there they were obviously still a family of much wealth and commercial importance in 1801. Detailed information about individuals of this family mentioned here and elsewhere has, however, been hard to find. The head of the family at this time seems to have been Grégoire Homberg (1740–1817). Henry Homberg appears to have been his nephew. The relation of Edward Homberg has not been determined (recent correspondence with the mayor of Le Havre). From Victor's business letters during his sojourn in France it appears that the Hombergs were doing business under the firm name of Veuve Homberg & Homberg Frères & Cie, or more simply Veuve Homberg Frères & Cie, with their principal office and warehouses in Le Havre. Their facilities were much used by Victor du Pont in the storage and shipping of goods to America, notably in handling the equipment for the projected powder mill on the Brandywine (V. du P. Letter Book—1801, passim, Winterthur MSS and Longwood MSS).

[23]MS Haver.   [24]MS says.

The 7th—we had a great din[n]er at our house, paid by the losings at cards during the passage. I was one of the winners.[25] It was not so merry a party as we expected, as those of the passengers who were detained by the municipality were greatly out of spirit.

Sunday 8th—I dined at Mr. Fouache['s],[26] a respectable old man, very handsome family; he was one of the richest merch[an]t[s] in Havre[27] before the Revolution but has lost great deal in Santo Domingo.[28]

The roads are not safe between this place and Paris. The stages are robbed almost every week. The Government obliges them to take a guard of five men on the top of their carriages though every body remonstrate against it, as it is certain that the diligences are stop'd more often since that measure—five men squeez'd in a basket and sleeping on their arms, which they cannot handle, being no match for gangs of 20 or 30 peasants, called Chouans.[29]

I was very much embarass'd what to do, having a great quantity of gold with me and not liking to exchange it with

---

[25]Victor was much given to gambling for small sums at various kinds of card games during his journey. The records of his winnings and losses are scattered widely over the recto pages of his *Pocket Remembrancer*. There is one summation of the whole record from Feb. 1801 through Dec. (?) which shows winnings of 594 livres and losses of 871 livres.

[26]A Fouache appears on a list of important merchants of Le Havre, drawn up in 1810, with an estimated fortune of between 500,000 and 800,000 francs. A note describes him as "des connaissances, du mérite, parlant et écrivant bien" (Étienne Dejean, *Un préfet du Consulat, Jacques-Claude Beugnot* [Paris, 1907], p. 311 and note). Whether or not he may be identified with Victor's host in 1801 is undetermined, but if not, he was probably of the same family.

[27]MS *Haver*.

[28]MS *St. Domingue*.

[29]Peasants of Brittany and Normandy who rose in revolt in 1793 against the government of the Terror. Their opposition was perhaps more religious than royalist. Their movement became merged with the counterrevolutionary rising in the Vendée.

loss against bills which might be bad and give a greater loss still. After a little hesitation I trusted chance and my good star. I took a post chaise with Mr. Hamon till Rouen, this kind of conveyance being much more respected by the Chouans than the diligence.

We left Havre[30] at 5 o'clock Monday morning. It was very dark. At the turnpike gate the keeper told us that[31] a Butcher had just been murdered on the top of the hill about a mile ahead. I confess I did not like much the information, but when my companion did insist upon turning back, his fears reviv'd my courage and I proved him that it was the very time to be safely on the road, as the men who had committed the act had certainly taken themselves out of the way. We arriv'd at Rouen for din[n]er without any accident. I could not find anybody in the evening, so we went to the play and saw a pretty vaudeville call'd La revue de l'an 9.

Tuesday 10th—the whole morning I visited merch[an]ts and saw Mr. Beugnot,[32] the prefe[c]t, who invited me to din[n]er. I did not know him but was acquainted of the circomstance of his having been a fellow prisoner with my father at the Force[33] under Robespierre. I never in my life met with a more cordial reception, nor experienc'd more

---

[30]MS *Haver*.   [31]MS *than*.

[32]Jacques Claude, Comte Beugnot (1761–1835). A moderate member of the Legislative Assembly, he was attacked by the Jacobin extremists and imprisoned in La Force during the Terror. In eclipse for a time under the Directory, he was back in favor during the Consulate and Empire. After several years as prefect of Rouen, he was made a member of the Council of State in 1806 and a count of the Empire in 1808. He was employed by Napoleon in various important capacities, yet survived the Emperor's downfall and continued in important public service under succeeding governments, but with diminishing influence.

[33]La Force, the famous Paris prison, in which du Pont de Nemours was confined from late July until late Aug. 1794. Jacques Claude, Comte Beugnot, in his *Mémoires* (ed. Comte Albert Beugnot, Paris, 1868, ch. vi) has left an account of their life there together in the closing days of the Terror.

pleasing sensations during my whole stay in France than I did
that day in hearing Mr. Beugnot speak of my father. He
loves him; he reverenc'd him; he adores him. There was a
large party at din[n]er, of generals, civil officers of the department, and some of the first people in Rouen. Mr. Beugnot,
who speaks very gracefully, entertain'd his company the
whole time with nothing but anecdotes[34] respecting my
father and sometimes brought the tears in my eyes. The
necessity of his returning to France was here as everywhere
the general chorus.

In the evening Mr. Beugnot carried me to an Assembly
of ladies. There was a cold supper, bouillote's[35] parties,
everything in the great stile as in Paris—some of the ladies
very handsome and very whimsically dress'd, that is to say
hiding their faces as much as possible with their hair and
long lace veils or Caps and shewing almost everything else.[36]
Though I saw the society of Rouen only that evening, I
thought I had seen enough[37] to conclude that the ladies did
not only dress, but did great many things else, as in Paris.
Few months after this I met Mr. B[eugnot] there, at a friend's
house and he said very gravely that there was not another
place in France like Rouen for modest[38] women.[39] I could
not with[h]old a laugh, as it brought me in mind that man
in the Scripture who could not see a beam in his own eye
but would see a mote in his neighbour's. My friend is a much
better man, for he cannot see the beam in his neighb[our's],
etc.—c'est une grace d'État.

I met at Mr. Beugnot['s] a daughter of Mr. Ed[ward] Hom-

---

[34]MS anectodes.

[35]A kind of very rapid brelan (a game resembling poker) for four
players.

[36]Two words have been struck out following else.

[37]Three words have been struck out following enough, and the
words to conclude have been substituted for them.

[38]One word has been struck out following modest.

[39]A whole sentence of five or six words has been struck out following women.

berg to whom he had given me an introduction. Her husband, Mr. Lambert,[40] was in Paris. She was covered with diamonds. I was very much surprised to hear her say after the parties were over, that it was very foolish to sit up so late every night, especially such [a] Day as the next being a post day, she must go to the store at 7 o'clock next morning in order to answer twenty letters and make several payments. I was ready to turn the thing as a jocke of hers when I heard another lady talk in the same manner. I then turned to a gentleman and asked him whether it was the custom in Rouen for ladies to attend the[41] counting houses and carry the business. He answered very politely that it was so, that the merchant's ladies were generaly book keepers or cashiers and sometimes had the direction of the whole house and trade. I asked him, with as much gravity as I could command, whether they would allow their husbands and clerks to make sweet meats and nurse the children. Then perceiving that I meant to ridicule, he said very peevishly, "No Sir, they won't even allow that," and turn'd his back upon me with as much contempt for my outlandish notions of good things as I had for his jerry countrymen and their breeches-wearing Spouses.

Wednesday 11th—I visited merchants and fabrics. I saw the *halle* or market, in which is sold every week all the linnen and other stuffs fabricated in the neighbouring country. I was surprised at the quantity of goods and more so when I heard that business was done there for 2 or three millions every market day. In fact this place and the whole province does not appear to have suffered so much by the war as one would naturally expect. The Country looks flourishing and in a state of high cultivation.

---

[40]In 1804–1805 a merchant of Rouen named Lambert was one of the twelve directors of the Banque de Rouen (Duverneuil and J. de La Tynna, *Almanach du commerce de Paris, des départemen[t]s de l'empire français et des principales villes de l'Europe,* An xiii [Paris, 1805], pp. 595, 596).

[41]Several letters have been deleted after *the.*

I went to Eauplette[42] to dine at my Cousin Pouchet-Belmare['s].[43] His house is large, in good order, and handsomely situated on the banks of the Seine. The gardens [are] laid out without any taste, *à la mode du pays*. I found there a dozen of relations, all very good people and very polite, as their grand fathers were 100 years ago. But the Ladies did look so knowing about trade and politics, and their husbands so convinced of their superiority in skill and judgement, that I soon percieved that my poor Co[u]sins were, as many of their fellow citizens of the town and suburbs, tame subjects of the Republic of Petticoats. I promised myself to mark Rouen in my memorandum book as the last place in the world where I will come to settle: I have a natural aversion to a woman of business as to a woman who takes snuff, and have no idea of the firms of Mothers Daughters Nurses & Co. I would sooner have married a complete Coquette than a complete merchant.

At eleven o'clock after supper we left Rouen—nine in a diligence, three in the outside and five soldiers on the top, and about 2000 lb. of bag[g]age. We went along as fast as 5 and sometimes 6 horses could drive us and consequently very slow.

I arrived in Paris Thursday 12th at 7 o'clock in the evening with Petit de Villers and Hamon. My brother had been gone some days before. We arrived in the rue Vivienne.[44] As soon as the diligence stopped I intended to run out in search of rooms at the Hotel de Boston or some other in the neighbour[h]ood, leaving my companions in the mean time to take care of my trunks; but [I] was immediately arrested by some people who shut the street door upon us. We were detained in that manner two hours till the director

[42]Eauplet-les-Rouen on the Seine, a short distance above Rouen.

[43]Pierre Abraham Pouchet-Belmare, an oilcloth manufacturer, born 6 Oct. 1762 (H. A. du Pont, *The Early Generations of the du Pont and Allied Families* [New York, 1923], I, 355–356).

[44]In central Paris, extending from the Palais-Royal northward.

of the Diligence had settled all his money concerns with every passenger, delivered the baggage etc., and had at last leisure to examine our passports, copy them, and receive a declaration respecting our business in Paris, the stay we meant to make there, and the place where we intended to lodge. I was very much vexed and out of humour at this tyranical behaviour to strangers. I had been 2 hours ruminating upon it and sighing for my dear America where the government does not trouble itself about private concerns; so I did answer to the 3 questions that *I did not know*. It was perfectly true as to the two last. The man threatened[45] to send me to the police, but I depended on my friends to be soon out of their claws. However I was wrong and promised myself afterwards not to behave so again. My friends made up for me with the man and at last we found ourselves at liberty to seek for lodgings. The hotels were all full and we were obliged to divide in three different houses. I went at the Hotel des Etrangers where I got a small dark room up in the fourth story.

I was fatigued and sick and found myself quite forlorn. My brother came to see me next morning and promised to look for lodgings where we could stay together. He had till then lodged with Harmand.[46] I got up to call on Mr. Bider-

[45]The word *me* has been struck out after *threatened*.

[46]Philippe Nicolas Harmand (1759–1838). Employed by du Pont de Nemours at his country estate Bois-des-Fossés in the 1780's as tutor to his sons, Victor and Irénée, he married a cousin of the first Mme du Pont de Nemours and remained in intimate friendship with the du Pont family throughout life. He was closely associated with du Pont de Nemours and Irénée in the printing business in Paris during the turbulent days of the French Revolution and was largely instrumental in the successful concealment of the former when he was under attack by the Jacobin extremists following the fall of the monarchy. He co-operated with the family in arranging for emigration to America and represented them in France after their departure. With their full approval he became the owner of Bois-des-Fossés. After the extremes of the Revolution had passed, he gained public employment and became director of the Pension Office of the National Treasury

man[n],[47] but I still had a very bad cold and a little fever. I kept my room two days, drank great deal of Limonade and the fever which had been pretty high during 24 hours left me.

Sunday I found myself well enough to dine with Mr. Roman.[48] I saw in the morning Messrs. de Marbois[49] and

---

(Life of E. I. du Pont, passim; see also Charles Poisson, *Les fournisseurs aux armées sous la Révolution française...*[Paris, 1932], pp. 39, 44, 45, 47n, 54n, 306).

[47]Jacques Bidermann (1751–1817), a Paris banker of Swiss origin, who was a close and loyal friend of du Pont de Nemours and his sons. He was one of the original investors in the firm of Du Pont de Nemours, Père et Fils & Cie and in the powder company. He was particularly helpful to E. I. du Pont when the latter went to Paris early in 1801 to acquire powder-making machinery and funds for his new enterprise. He was the father of James Antoine Bidermann, who came to America in 1814 and was to play an important part in the du Pont family and business during the next generation (B. G. du Pont, *Du Pont de Nemours 1739–1817* [2 vols.; Newark, Del., 1933], *passim; Life of E. I. du Pont, passim;* see also Poisson, *op. cit., passim).*

[48]Little is known of him except what can be gathered from the documentary collections in the Eleutherian Mills Historical Library. He is mentioned in the prospectus of the firm of Du Pont de Nemours, Père et Fils & Cie (1800) as a partner in the Paris firm of Gros d'Avilliers & Cie, who was acting in a secretarial capacity to the Du Pont Company: "The citizen Roman, one of their partners, will pay the dividends to our shareholders, and will always be able to give them any information they may want concerning our affairs and our situation." He long continued in close friendship with the du Ponts and with the Bidermanns *(Life of E. I. du Pont, passim;* Poisson, *op. cit., passim).*

[49]François Barbé-Marbois (1745–1837), the well-known diplomat and functionary who is principally famous for having negotiated on Napoleon's part the treaty by which Louisiana was ceded to the United States. As French consul general he had resided in the U.S. for some ten years before being appointed intendant of Santo Domingo in 1783. Back in France during the Revolution, he was deported to French Guiana as a royalist in 1797. He was released by Bonaparte, who made him councilor of State and director of the Treasury in 1801

Johannot.[50] I moved [to the] Hotel de Paris, rue de Richelieu, with Irenée and Petit de Villers.

Monday 16th—I paid a visit to Consul Le Brun[51] who
lives in the Queen's appartements in the Tuileries. He
admitted me instantly and kept me to dine. I found there
many of my father's friends all regretting very much his
absence. Everybody was covered with laces and embroidery,
Counsellors of State, Prefe[c]ts, Judges, members of the Institute. Everybody is in uniform. It is a very natural thing
under a military government and it appears to render men
more confident and proud of their own dignity and merit.
It is surprising to see how every man is turn[ed] a Courtier
since there is a court; for this present government is the
first since the Revolution which has affected to copy the
ancient regime, its politeness, its splendor, its dignity.

Next day I was invited to a great *fête* Mr. Talleyrand gave
to the first Consul to celebrate his victories in Italy and
the peace with the Emperor.[52] It was the most magnificent

---

and senator in 1802. Changing his political principles with successive
governments, he managed to remain in Napoleon's later service as
president of the Cour des Comptes and to continue in that office under
Louis XVIII (E. W. Lyon, *The Man Who Sold Louisiana* [Norman,
Okla., 1942]). He was one of the early subscribers to the firm of Du
Pont de Nemours, Père et Fils & Cie but drew back from paying all
that he had promised.

[50] Jean Johannot (1748–1829), a Paris investor and businessman of
Swiss origin. He had been a member of the National Convention
(representing the department of Haut-Rhin) and of the Council of
Ancients. Retiring from political life in 1797, he became a rope
manufacturer in Vaucresson (near Paris) and mayor of that village
in 1799 (Kuscinski, *Dictionnaire des conventionnels*). He was interested
in Du Pont de Nemours, Père et Fils & Cie to the extent of five shares
and also in the powder company.

[51] Charles François Lebrun (1739–1834) was Third Consul, along
with Cambacérès and Bonaparte, and owed his appointment to the
latter.

[52] The Treaty of Lunéville (9 Feb. 1801) between France and Austria,

thing of the kind I ever saw. There is in the Foreign Affairs's hotel[53] a long gallery with a theatre appropriated to
this sort of days; but nevertheless the appartements were not
sufficiently large and the only fault I found was the crowd.
It began with a concert in which Mrs. Grassini,[54] an Italian
Lady or rather *Cantatrice,* displaid all the charms of a most
delicious voice. She is a very handsome woman and had
more diamonds on her neck, head, breast and arms than I
remember to have seen to any woman before. It was reported
that Bonaparte gave her part of these diamonds in Italy
where he had a fancy to her; and I[55] remarked that he seemed
very much pleased during her singing and Madame Bonaparte[56] quite out of humor; for she is very jealous though
her husband does not give her any subject. Mde Bonaparte
was very plainly dressed, brown silk gown and her hair tied
à la Grecque, but her diamonds[57] very large. Diamond[s]
are very much the fashion now and very abondant since
Generals and Commissaries of the government get them so
cheap. After the concert the Company were conducted in[to]
the gallery where the players of the Vaudeville[58] performed

following upon the victories of Marengo and Hohenlinden (14 June
and 3 Dec. 1800).

[53] The Hôtel Galliffet, the seat of the Ministry of Foreign Affairs,
in the rue du Bac, which extends southward from the Pont Royal
through the faubourg St. Germain.

[54] Joséphine Grassini (1773–1850), the Italian contralto who rose
to fame in Italy in 1794, or soon after, and remained a reigning
favorite, particularly in Paris and London, until the close of the
Napoleonic era.

[55] The words *Diamonds are much the fashion now* (constituting
almost a whole line) have been struck out after *I* (see Introduction,
p. xix).

[56] Marie Josèphe Rose Tascher de la Pagerie, called Josephine
(1763–1814), a native of Martinique. At the time of her marriage to
Bonaparte, she was the widow of General Alexandre, Vicomte de
Beauharnais, who had been guillotined during the Reign of Terror.

[57] The word *were* has been struck out after *diamonds.*

[58] The Théâtre de Vaudeville, on the rue de Chartres-Saint-Honoré,
established in 1782.

a little comedy wrote on the subject of peace, in which almost every verse was a praise of Bonaparte and even Mrs. Bonaparte, [and] Miss Beauharnais,[59] her brother,[60] in fact the whole of the Royal family. There were[61] also some words in favor of General Moreau[62] and some others. After the play the best dancers of the Opera performed a quadrille or ballet in which they represented all the crowned[63] heads of Europe in their great State Dress—the two Emperors,[64] the Great Turck[65] and the Pope dancing hand in hand. I thought it was a very foolish idea, especially as the Austrian, the Russian, and the Prussian minister[s] were present, and I suppose they really felt awkward in seeing the Caricatures of their masters, dressed with Stars and ribbons very much like themselves, kicking and capering about the Room. The contredances and Walses began as soon as this ballet was over. It is surprising to see to what height the art of dancing is carried now in France. Young people appear[66] to have done nothing else in their life: in fact it is the same steps as the dancers perform on the stage and it becomes too formal to be pleasant, too difficult to be agreable even to the byestanders. The ladies do[67] not vie now, who will dress the most but rather who will undress. I have never seen such display of human flesh. Their arms are nacked up to the armpit, their breast[s] entirely uncovered and their shoulders bare

---

[59]Hortense de Beauharnais (1783–1837), daughter of Alexandre and Josephine de Beauharnais. In 1802 she married Louis Bonaparte (King of Holland, 1806–1810), and bore him a son who became Napoleon III.

[60]Eugène de Beauharnais (1781–1824), son of Alexandre and Josephine de Beauharnais. As a general he served ably in the campaigns of his stepfather Napoleon, who made him viceroy of Italy in 1805.

[61]MS *was.*

[62]General Jean Victor Moreau (1763–1813), the hero of Hohenlinden.

[63]MS *crowns.*

[64]I.e., the Holy Roman Emperor and the Czar of Russia.

[65]The Sultan of the Ottoman Empire.

[66]MS *appears.*

[67]MS *does.*

below the middle of their backs. The tails of their gowns are extremely long but the petticoats very short, and they have only one or two, and very thin to expose all the shape of their limbs. During the Ball Bonaparte kept walking from one room into another. Four aides de Camps were always with him; two walk'd behind and two before. They are tall handsome young men[68] in hussard dress, covered with Gold and the feather of their caps as high as the ceiling. Some officers of his body guards, some of his ministers surrounded him; and Talleyrand dandling along on his lame feet kept close, to do the honours of the *fête*.

Every body was making room for Bonaparte with every appearance of respect and adulation. He was constantly bowing on each side of the row and stopp'd sometimes to speak two or three words. He kept constantly smiling, but you could plainly see that it is not a natural motion for his features, and if smile was on his lips Care and melancholie were hanging on his eyebrows. The fact is that since the attempts on his life he has been constantly depressed and agitated. I had a very fair view of him, having General La Fayette under my arm[69] when he stop'd to ask him how he did and if he had news from his son. (Washington La Fayette[70] had been severely wounded at a late affair in Italy under G[ener]al Rochambeau.)[71] It was that evening that I saw Mr. La Fayette for the first time since June 1791.[72] He know'd me first; came to me and shook me warmly by the hand, saying "Don't you know me Victor."[73] I stood amazed, recollecting his voice, a little

---

[68]The word *dressed* has been struck out after *men*.

[69]MS *harm*.

[70]George Washington Motier de La Fayette (1799–1849), eldest son of General La Fayette.

[71]Donatien Marie Joseph de Vimeur, Vicomte de Rochambeau (1750–1813), son of the Comte de Rochambeau who was commander of the French forces in America during the Revolutionary War.

[72]When Victor was aide-de-camp to La Fayette, commander of the National Guard in the French Revolution.

[73]Several illegible letters have been struck out after *Victor*.

Every body was making room for Bonaparte
with every appearance of respect & adulation
he was constantly bowing on each side of the
row & stopp'd sometimes to speak two or
three words, he kept constantly smiling but
you could plainly see that it is not a natural
motion for his features & if smile was on
his lips Care & melancholic anxiety were
hanging on his eyebrows. the fact is that
since the attempts on his life he has been
constantly depressed & agitated; I had a very
fair view of him having General lafayette
under my harm when he stop'd to ask him
how he did & if he had news from his son.
(Washington lafayette had been severely
wounded at a late affair in italy under Gal
Rochambeau) It was that evening that I
saw Mr. Lafayette for the first time since
June 1791 — he know'd me first came to me
& shook me warmly by the hand saying don't
you know me Victor, I stood amased
recollecting his voice a little his features but
not being able to command my astonishment at
seeing him looking so young, he embraced
me a dozen times with the most fatherly
tenderness, I had fancied to myself that
seven years confinement would have had the
same effect on him which they had on Pusy
who looks so much older, Mrs lafayette

FACSIMILE OF A PAGE OF THE MANUSCRIPT

his features, but not being able to command my astonishment at seeing him looking so young. He embraced me a
dozen times with the most fatherly tenderness. I had fancied
to myself that seven years confinement would have had the
same effect on him which they had on Puzy[74] who looks so
much older. But La Fayette looks certainly much younger
than he did 10 years ago, in fact younger than myself. He
has grown fat, he wears a brown wig and it makes in him
the greatest alteration. I was very happy to meet him and
staid with him the whole evening.

At one o'clock every body walked downstairs to supper.
The stair case was beautifully lighted and decorated with
flower pots, the whole wall being covered with them as a
bower; and the flowers in full blossom as in the middle of
summer perfumed the air. The supper was dressed in four
large rooms. After some music Mr. Esmangard,[75] who is a
kind of Poet laureat attached to the Ministry of the Interior,
recitated to Bonaparte an Ode of his composition. It was
the most glaring piece of flattery that was ever composed.
Demigods, heroes, philosophers, Emperors of the past, present, and future times were ninnies in comparison with the

---

[74]Jean Xavier Bureaux de Pusy (1750–1806), son-in-law of the
second Mme du Pont de Nemours. Like du Pont de Nemours, he had
been a member of the National Constituent Assembly. As an army
engineer of distinction he had served on the staff of La Fayette and
with the General had been arrested by the Austrians in 1792 and
imprisoned at Olmütz. He had been released in 1797 under the terms
of the Treaty of Campo Formio on condition that he should not
return to France. In May 1799, several months in advance of the main
family migration, he sailed from Rotterdam for New York with his
daughter Sara and Mme du Pont de Nemours. He returned to France
and public life there upon Bonaparte's rise to power.

[75]Not otherwise identified. It seems not improbable that the author
has fallen into confusion here and that the poet in question should
be Joseph Alphonse Esménard (1770–1811), best known for his poem
entitled "La navigation." His life of many vicissitudes brought him
to temporary favor in Paris just at this time when he was named
Chef du Bureau des Théâtres in the Ministry of the Interior.

General. I am sure Lewis the 14th nor any despot[76] of the East have ever been so much adulated, and I am surprised how any man who may like to see these things in print, can bear to hear it told to his face. However the first Consul did not blush at all; he took it kindly as his due, and as he look'd very much please[d], every body else ought to have been so.

Some of the company did not arrive[77] before 6 o'clock in the morning, and it would have been nearly my lot had not the man who drove my cabriolet been a dashing fellow. At 10 o'clock I arrived at the *Pont Royal,* where the file of carriages began, with soldiers to prevent you to break it. I had been half an hour to advance twenty yards when Consular guards galloping away announced the Carriage of Bonaparte, his family, and the other Consuls. My fellow fi[n]ding his chance to get in between Mde Bonaparte's and Cambaceres's carriages, pushed in and kept whipping and galloping till we arrived at the foot of the stairs in Talleyrand's yard— where I crept out, very much effrayed to be seen by the guards who must have taken me at least for the Secretary of State or some such thing.

Next day dining with Reveroni[78] it was remarked with wonder that some[79] could not get in before the morning. At all these feasts, though the greatest care was taken to prevent confusion in the carriages, when taking my pencil[80] I soon calculated that it could not be otherwise. There are[81] 1200 persons asked and, though they do not all go, many slide in without cards of invitation, so it is about the number; supposing three to arrive in each carriage, which is

---

[76]MS *despost.*   [77]MS *arriv'd.*

[78]MS *Reverony.* Jacques Antoine Reveroni de Saint-Cyr (1767– 1829), a military engineer and prolific writer not only on scientific subjects but of plays and romances. He was a son-in-law of the second Mme du Pont de Nemours. Several of his works were published by the Du Pont Press.

[79]Several illegible letters have been struck out after *some.*

[80]MS *pincel.*   [81]MS *is.*

rather more than the average, and giving only one minute and [a] half to each carriage to arrive before the door, unload, and make room for another, it requires 10 hours; so if the first company gets in at 9 o'clock, the last cannot possibly be arrived before 7 o'clock the next morning.

Thursday 19th—I dined with Mr. de Lessert,[82] where I met Lusignan,[83] Portalis,[84] and many other of my father's friends. I dined constantly at this house, once every week—the Sunday or the Decadi.[85]

---

[82]Étienne Delessert (1735–1816), a Paris banker and businessman who had been imprisoned during the period of revolutionary violence but had been released after the fall of Robespierre. He is especially notable for his interest in agriculture and breeding and for his part in introducing Spanish Merino sheep into France. He had a holding of 1800 acres near Kingston, N.Y., on the Hudson River and co-operated with E. I. du Pont in bringing Merino sheep to this country in 1801 (James Mease, *Archives of Useful Knowledge* [Philadelphia, 1811], I, 103–106; *Life of E. I. du Pont, passim*).

[83]Perhaps an error for Luzignem, i.e., Hugues Thibault Henri Jacques, Marquis de Luzignem (1753–1815), "chevalier de Saint Louis, mestre de camp commandant du régiment de Flandre-infanterie." A representative of the Noblesse of Paris in the States General, he was one of the first of his order to side with the Third Estate in the formation of the National Assembly. A friendship with du Pont de Nemours would have been natural at this time. Later he became alarmed at the revolutionary excesses, sold his properties, and went abroad, where he engaged in successful speculation. Upon the rise of Bonaparte to power in 1800, he returned to Paris and made a vain attempt to gain a place for himself in the Senate. He would have been of interest to Victor du Pont as a potential investor in the du Pont enterprises.

[84]Jean Étienne Marie Portalis (1746–1807), a distinguished jurist of conservative or moderate sympathies who, as a member of the Council of Ancients, opposed the Directory in its later excesses and was obliged to go into exile. With the rise of Bonaparte to power he returned to Paris and was made a member of the Council of State and director of ecclesiastical affairs. He played major parts in the drafting of the Civil Code and in the conclusion of the Concordat of 1801 with the Papacy.

[85]The tenth day of the decade in the French Republican calendar.

[31]

The 20th—I dined with the good, amiable and always handsome Mrs. de Rumilly.[86] She is of all the women I know the one whose manners and kind of beauty I am the most fond of; and she is also of all the ladies of my acquaintance the one to whom I have been the less attentive,[87] and even the less polite. It is a kind of bashfullness I cannot account for, except it might be the consciousness of my becoming too much in love with her, if once I had broken the ice.

Brousse[88] was there and the·Director of the sail cloath manufactory at Angers,[89] with whom I had a long conference respecting what could be done for the sale of their cloath in the United States.

---

[86]Mme Auriol de Rumilly. Information concerning her is very limited. A letter which she wrote to Victor du Pont, 20 Aug. 1802, is signed "Auriol de Rumilly." She was evidently a close friend of his wife, and she had a small house at Brévannes, near Corbeil south of Paris and not far from the residence of Monsieur Brousse. In a letter to his wife, 25 Aug. 1801, he writes: " Il y a deux jou͞r͞ ͞m͞a chère, que j'ai été diner à Brévannes chez M͞ʳ. Brouss͞e. . ͡ ͞ ͞ bonne et d ͡ ͞ Mde de Rumilly a acheté une petite maison ͜ ͡ͺ face qu'elle ᵗᵃᶦᵗ arranger et qui sera fort jolie.... Elle se porte mieuͫ͞ que ja͞m͞ ͺͦ (V. du P. to Mme V. du P., 25 Aug. 1801, Winterthur MSS). S]͡ ͡ͻ mentioned several times in Mme du Pont's letters to her husband. In one of these, 1 May 1801, she reminds him of commissions he and Mme de Rumilly are to execute for Mrs. [Gabriel] M[anigault?] (Mme V. du P. to V. du P., 1 May 1801, Winterthur MSS). In 1802 Mme de Rumilly appears to be the sender of a box in which du Pont de Nemours was forwarding a number of documents, circulars, newspapers, books, and the like from France, to be distributed between his sons upon arrival in New York (Life of E. I. du Pont, VI, 125).

[87]By a slip the word to has been added after attentive.

[88]Brousse, who lived at Brévannes and was a friend of Mme de Rumilly, has not been further identified. Victor du Pont saw him frequently, usually at dinner (see pp. 43, 54, 105, 107, 112).

[89]The sailcloth manufactory in question was the firm of Bonnaire Joubert Girard & Cie, which later offered to send samples to Victor du Pont (their letter to Du Pont de Nemours, Père et Fils & Cie. 21 April 1801, Winterthur MSS).

21st—All the morning[90] I employed in seeing my father's friends and carrying the letters I brought for them. I dined with Mde de Stael;[91] there was a large Company, as there is always every *duodi*,[92] and a strange mixture of men of all parties. Mde de Stael is now at the head of the opposition party and patronize[s] the few members of the Tribunate[93] who like Chenier[94] and some other[s] dare speak against the measures of the Government and oppose the laws urged on by the Council of State.[95] This opposition is very weak in number[s] but not in Courage; and really it requires now as much courage to oppose the will of the gold and steel-bright and powerfull Sovereignty as[96] it did in any other moment of the Revolution to [97] displease the mob of the Ragamuffins *sans Culotes*—especially as it is known that the Consul, who has not let aside yet his military habits, cannot bear contradiction nor opposition. It is reported that,[98] speaking the oth-

---

[90]MS *mornings.*

[91]Anne Louise Germaine Necker, Baronne de Staël-Holstein (1766–1817), daughter of Jacques Necker and a political and literary figure of the epoch whose importance requires no comment. She was then living on the rue de Grenelle in the faubourg St. Germain.

[92]The second day of the decade in the French Republican calendar.

[93]One of the two lower houses of the legislature under the Consulate (Constitution of the year VIII). Its function was to discuss or debate proposed legislation before members of the Legislative Body, whose duty it was to vote.

[94]Marie Joseph Blaise de Chénier (1764–1811), brother of the more famous poet, André de Chénier. A poet and dramatist of distinction, he was an important political figure, being successively a member of the Convention, the Council of Five Hundred, and the Tribunate (Kuscinski, *Dictionnaire des conventionnels*).

[95]A constitutional body whose members were nominated by Bonaparte, the First Consul, and which was much used by him. Its principal function was to initiate legislation.

[96]MS *than.*

[97]Several illegible letters have been struck out after *to.*

[98]MS *than.*

er day of the special tribunals law,[99] which has been so long debated by the Tribunate he said, *"Si ces bougres-là* have not done with it this decade I'll have everyone of them into the Temple.[100] I believe they take me for a fool of a king and mean[101] to act [as] a remonstrating parliament." The Consul does not like Mde de Stael and she has broken with Talleyrand who treats her very ill and did not even ask[102] her to his fête.

The 22d—Being a tridi,[103] I dined at Mr. Biderman[n's], as I do every tridi, to meet my father['s] old friends who are all very fond to talk of him—among many other[s], Maret,[104] the Secretary of State, General du Pont,[105] Mejan,[106] Secre-

---

[99]As a part of the repressive régime following the attempt to assassinate the First Consul, 24 Dec. 1800, a law was enacted, 7 Feb. 1801, which empowered the government to establish in local departments where they were deemed necessary special criminal courts *(tribunaux criminels spéciaux),* partly military and partly civil, which were to function without juries and without appeal and which could impose any penalty, including death. The proposed law encountered strong opposition in the Tribunate, where it was debated for more than a fortnight before passage (Ernest Lavisse, ed., *Histoire de France contemporaine* [Paris, 1921], III, 76).

[100]One of the well-known prisons of revolutionary Paris (a survival of the ancient fortified monastery of the Knights Templars), it is particularly famous as the place where Louis XVI and his family were incarcerated.

[101]MS *meant.*   [102]MS *ask'd.*

[103]The third day of the decade in the French Republican calendar.

[104]Hughes Bernard Maret (1763–1839). A successful lawyer and moderate supporter of the Revolution, he is remembered as the man who initiated the *Bulletin de l'Assemblée Nationale,* which became the *Moniteur universel.* Upon the rise of Bonaparte to power he became one of his most devoted supporters. Beginning as Bonaparte's secretary, he was soon made secretary of state. He was made a count in 1807 and Duke of Bassano in 1809.

[105]Pierre Antoine Dupont de l'Étang (1765–1840). He rose rapidly in the Army during the Revolution, but his principal fame was achieved in the Napoleonic wars.

[106]Étienne Méjan (1766–1846). He co-operated with Maret in the

tary General of the Prefecture of Paris, l'Abbé Morellet,[107] and some members of the National Institute.

Monday the 23d—I dined at Mr. Lang['s],[108] a late partner of the house of Lang Hupet & Gelot, bankers, doing great deal with the Government. Mr. Lang is a great Epicure. I spent the evening at my friend Tilden['s][109] of Boston who

---

establishment of the *Bulletin de l'Assemblée Nationale*. A moderate supporter of the Revolution, he withdrew from political life during the Terror but became active once more after the fall of Robespierre and collaborated with du Pont de Nemours in the journal entitled *L'historien*. With the rise of Bonaparte to power, he became secretary general of the Seine. Later he enjoyed an important post under Prince Eugène in Italy.

[107]Abbé André Morellet (1727–1819), the well-known economist and writer, closely associated with the philosophes and physiocrats.

[108]In 1800 and 1801 he was involved with the firm of Du Pont de Nemours, Père et Fils & Cie in a speculation in batistes (*Life of E. I. du Pont,* V, 134, 260, 312).

[109]David Tilden, Jr. (1773–1847), a son of David Tilden (1741–1814), of Boston. In a series of letters from him to Victor du Pont (Winterthur MSS), it appears that he was serving as supercargo on the brig *Mary* of Boston (Capt. Southworth) which had sailed from Charleston, S.C., in April 1797 for Bordeaux. He had arrived in Bordeaux at the end of May, discharged and sold his cargo, and, reinvesting the proceeds in brandy, had started for Boston in August. Battered by a storm, Tilden had put in at the port of St. Martin, Ile de Ré, intending to go on to Boston. But his papers were found not to be in order, and he had been detained for more than eighteen months. Victor du Pont had assisted him with the French authorities in his effort to obtain justice and had even lent him 1,200 livres, a loan which was repaid in America by the victim's father in 1800 (D. Tilden, Jr., and D. Tilden, Sr., to V. du P., 1799–1800, Winterthur MSS). The dates of the Tildens given above are taken from "Linzee's manuscript Tilden Genealogy" preserved in the New England Historic Genealogical Society, Boston, Mass. This authority has no record of the marriage of David Tilden, Jr., and his will, dated 1847, makes no mention of either wife or children. He would have been 26 or 27 years old when, according to Victor du Pont, he married "the old and good Mde Tully."

married during my absence the old and good Mde Tully.[110]
She is pretty well at Court and with the ministers, through
her relationship with Mde Bonaparte.

Thursday 24th—I went with Mr. Biderman[n] to see
Mr. Ouvrard[111] upon business. He was absent and we waited
for him and took that opportunity to examine his house
which is one of the most curious things to be seen in Paris
for a stranger. It is furnish'd in the new Grecian and Egyp-
tian stile, and every refinement of luxury, every display of
wealth is found there. Many English improvements are also
introduced. In a word it is perfection itself and it would
require volumes to describe it. The splendour of Versaille[s]
and Trianon was nothing in comparison. This Mr. Ou-

[110]Information about this mysterious figure has been hard to obtain.
In M. L. E. Moreau de Saint-Méry, *Voyage aux États-Unis de l'Amérique, 1793–1798,* ed. S. L. Mims (New Haven, 1913), p. 248, we read
under the date of 16 Sept. 1797, "Mde Tully de la Martinique vint
nous voir." This was in Philadelphia. In Paris she appears more than
once in the pages of Victor's journal as Mrs. Tilden, and it is evident
that because of her influence or supposed influence with the French
government, he found it advantageous to cultivate her friendship
(see pp. 47, 99, 103, 107, 112). In his Day Book, Expences, such entries
as the following occur: 13 July "Nosegay for Mrs Tilden ... 4 [livres]
10"; 3 Oct. "Eventails for M[rs] T[ilden] ... 30"; and on p. 54 of this
same document he has brought together more serious outlays for her
as follows:

Mrs. Tilden acc[oun]t for the Marine	240
D[itt]o in a pin	30
Gown	27
D[itt]o silk	48
In cash	150
	495

[111]Gabriel Julien Ouvrard (1770–1846), a well-known, not to say
notorious, millionaire of the epoch. By great financial talent and
daring speculation and by contracts with the French government, he
gained an enormous fortune; but he was repeatedly the subject of
attacks by the government, notably by Napoleon (who also profited
greatly by his help), and ended his life in comparative obscurity in
London (*Mémoires de G.-J. Ouvrard, sur sa vie et ses opérations
financières* ...[3 vols.; Paris, 1826–27]).

vra[r]d I have known in 1795. Arriving from Nantes[112] without a shilling in the world, he has been, through Mde
Tallien[113] under Barras,[114] and through Mde Bonaparte
since, *fournisseur* general of the Marine and it is said he is
worth now 8 or ten millions. However he is borrowing money
at 2¼% [?] a month, and very likely shall soon be a bankrupt. He is no more in favor now, as he refused lending
money to Bonaparte to bribe the Directorial guards and effect the 18th of Brumaire.[115] It is Michel brothers[116] of Orleans who have advanced it. They and Collaud,[117] who has
known Bonaparte in Italy, are to succeed Ouvrard shortly in
the contracts for supplies. This house of Ouvrard has been

---

[112]MS *Nantz.*

[113]Thérésa Cabarrús Tallien (1773–1835), a notorious social and
political figure of the epoch. Of Spanish origin, she was the divorced
wife of the Marquis de Fontenay. From 1793 until 1795 she had a
marked influence on the course of the Revolution through the favor
she enjoyed with Jean Lambert Tallien (1767–1821), whom she married
in 1794. Thereafter she exercised a strong influence, first with Barras,
a leading member of the Directory, and then with Mme Bonaparte.

[114]Paul François Nicolas, Comte de Barras (1755–1829). Though
of noble family, he supported the Revolution and became a prominent
Jacobin. However, he turned against Robespierre, was a leading figure
in the Thermidorian reaction and under the Directory, and was in
part responsible for the rise of Bonaparte to power.

[115]The coup d'état (9 Nov. 1799) which brought Bonaparte to power.

[116]A Veuve Michel is listed among the commercial houses in Orléans
in 1804–1805 (Duverneuil and La Tynna, *Almanach du commerce,*
An XIII, p. 574).

[117]Conceivably General Jean Jacques Bernardin Colaud de la Salcette (1759–1834). (See Georges Six, *Dictionnaire biographique des
généraux & amiraux français de la Révolution et de l'Empire, 1792–
1814* [Paris, 1934], under "La Salcette"). After a distinguished career in
Italy and the Balkans, he was captured at Nicopolis in 1798 by the
Turks and held a prisoner until March 1801, after which he returned
to France, where he was placed on inactive duty for a time. This would
have been later than the period of the journal; but du Pont's account
of the career of Ouvrard seems to indicate that he may have been
writing from memory some time after the event. An anachronism with
respect to Colaud, therefore, might not be surprising.

sold since to the Chevalier de Azara,[118] Spanish ambassador, for three hundred and fifty thousand dollars payable in Vera Cruz.

The 25th—I dined with my old acquaintance Henry Waddel of Philadelphia who is still in the same predicament, solliciting the Government for the recovery of the money taken on board the Pigou.[119] There is a fine Society of Americans now in Paris, many of my old friends, as Henry Grant[120] of Charleston who, in spite of his title of American

---

[118]MS *Azzara*. Don José Nicolás de Azara (1730–1804) was a wealthy Spanish diplomat, art collector, and patron of artists. During a long residence as ambassador in Rome he assembled a distinguished collection. His efforts to save Rome from occupation by French forces in 1796 proved vain, and later he became ambassador to France.

[119]Though Henry Waddel has not been identified, the episode of the American armed merchantman *Pigou* (Capt. Green) is known. Sailing from Philadelphia in the autumn of 1798 and carrying, among other things, $150,000, she was captured six days after leaving the Delaware River by two French frigates, the specie was confiscated, and the ship was taken to Lorient. The ship was apparently liberated by June 1799, notwithstanding Victor's statement that the confiscated money was still being sought in 1801 (*Naval Documents Related to the Quasi-War between the U.S. and France, 1797–1801,* prepared by the Office of Naval Records [Washington, D.C., 1935–1938], I, 379–380; II, 185, 203, 273; III, 75). On the plight of American vessels and captains taken by French privateers in this period, see the printed letter of Victor du Pont, dated Paris, 9 Jan. 1799, to Citizen Abrial, commissary of the Executive Directory to the Tribunal de Cassation (Eleuthera Bradford du Pont Collection, Eleutherian Mills Historical Library). Waddel was still in Paris on terms of close friendship with Victor du Pont in the following Aug. and Sept. (see pp. 105, 108), and there is a record in his Classified Expense Account of an outlay for the christening of a Waddel child.

[120]More commonly *Hary* Grant. In a letter by Robert G. Harper to the U.S. Secretary of State, Pickering, recommending Grant's appointment to the consulship in London, he is described as a merchant, long resident in Charleston though presently in Philadelphia, and having connections in London as a partner in the firm of Shawn Mackenzie (Robert G. Harper to Timothy Pickering, 18 Nov. 1797, Applications

Consul in Scotland, was put in the Temple and detain'd there few days after the plot of the 3d of Nivose.[121] He was so much effrayed that nothing short[122] of the delight he takes in a Parisian life can reconcile him with the chance of going there again.

In the evening tea at Mde Lavoisier['s][123] and [a] ball at Mr. Biderman[n's].

The 26th—I dined with my friend De L'Orme[124] and early, in order to be able to go to the play afterwards. They

---

and Recommendations for Office, file on Hary Grant, Records of the Dept. of State, National Archives). He was appointed consul at Leith, Scotland, 14 July 1798. On 25 March 1805, Secretary of State Madison instructed James Monroe, American minister to Great Britain, to inform the British government and Hary Grant that the President had revoked Grant's commission on the ground that he had spent very little time at his assigned post (James Madison to James Monroe, 25 March 1805, Instructions to U.S. Ministers, Records of the Dept. of State, National Archives). In April 1799 Grant wrote Victor du Pont from London to congratulate him on his safe arrival in France, to tell him of the appointment of American envoys to negotiate peace with the French government, and to report his own misfortune in having his ships, the *Ann* and the *Susan* from Charleston, confiscated and taken into French ports. He desired to go over to France and try to make recovery, but he was afraid of capture unless du Pont could arrange a safe passage and would send him a pass (Hary Grant to V. du P., 6 April 1799, Winterthur MSS; see also p. 48).

[121]See p. 15, n. 12.   [122]MS *shorter*.

[123]Mme Antoine L. Lavoisier, the widow of the eminent French chemist who had taught the art of powder making to E. I. du Pont. A woman of remarkable versatility, social grace, and talent, she had shared largely in her husband's work. Greatly admired by du Pont de Nemours, she received from him, and rejected, a proposal of marriage not long after the execution of her husband.

[124]MS *De Lorme*. Presumably Marion De L'Orme who in 1785 and 1786 was the traveling companion of young Victor when he was sent by his father on two extended journeys through the provinces to report on the state of the French manufactories. He is mentioned frequently in the correspondence between father and son at that time, usually with the simple appellation "De L'Orme" but occasionally with the

dine now so late in Paris that you cannot generally get there
[i.e., to the play] before it is two-thirds over. In some houses
you do not sit down before half after seven and the usual
hour is six o'clock. We went to the Italians[125] where we saw
a new opera call'd L'irato.[126] It is a delightfull music from
Mehul. This is my favorite spectacle. They have charming
new operas in the style of the *Prison[n]ier*,[127] *l'opera
comique*,[128] *L'oncle valet*.[129] They are *Le calife de Bag-
dat*,[130] *La maison a vendre*,[131] and many other[s] I have not
yet seen.

---

extended form "Marion De L'Orme" (V. du P. to his father, 1785,
passim, Winterthur MSS). De L'Orme was a former silk manufacturer
from Lyons, who appears on a list of the office staff of du Pont
de Nemours when he was Inspector General of Commerce (1785–1787),
as "Sous-chef, chargé de ce qui regarde la balance du commerce …"
("Bureau de Mr. Du Pont" [1787], Winterthur MSS). When the
traveling companions arrived in Lyons in Aug. 1785, they stopped
for a time with the De L'Orme family (V. du P. to his father, 31 Aug.
1785, Winterthur MSS).

[125]The Théâtre des Italiens, the original of the Opéra-Comique,
from which the boulevard des Italiens takes its name.

[126]*L'irato; ou, L'emporté*, comic opera in one act; words by Benoît
Joseph Marsollier (1750–1817), music by Étienne Nicolas Méhul (1763–
1817); first presented, 17 Feb. 1801.

[127]*Le prisonnier, ou La ressemblance*, comic opera in one act; words
by Alexandre Duval (1767–1842), music by Dominique Dellamaria
(1768–1800); presented at the Théâtre Feydeau, 29 Jan. 1798.

[128]No satisfactory explanation has been found of the phrase *l'opéra
comique* as used here. It could be conceived as a description of *Le
prisonnier*, but it would have applied equally well to any of the other
comic operas which the author lists here.

[129]*L'oncle valet*, comic opera in one act, by the author and com-
poser of *Le prisonnier* mentioned above; presented, 8 Dec. 1798.

[130]*Le calife de Bagdad*, comic opera in one act; words by C. Godard
d'Aucour, Baron de Saint-Just (1769–1826), music by François Adrien
Boieldieu (1775–1834); said to have run through more than 800 per-
formances.

[131]*La maison à vendre*, comic opera in one act; words by Alexandre
Duval, music by Nicolas Dalayrac (1753–1809); presented 23 Oct. 1800.

VIEW OF THE BOULEVARDS (PARIS) FROM THE THEATRE DES ITALIENS WESTWARD
From an anonymous lithograph in Musée Carnavalet, Paris.

The 27th—I went to dine with Irenéé and Lamotte[132] at Pevre['s],[133] one of my comrades, aide de camp of La Fayette. We met four at the General['s] one morning— Romeuf, Curmer,[134] Peyre and me.

Saturday 28th—I spent the day at Mad. de la Rochefoucault['s],[135] the wife of Mr. Short,[136] for she does not yet take his name though lawfully married to him. There was Mr. and Mrs. La Fayette, Mr. and Mrs. Latour-Maubourg.[137]

[132]Charles Antoine Houdar de Lamotte (1763–1806), a cousin of du Pont de Nemours' sons.

[133]Antoine Marie Peyre (1770–1843), distinguished architect and patriot. He had been associated with Victor and Irénée du Pont in the National Guard under La Fayette.

[134]Romeuf and Curmer were aides-de-camp in the National Guard under La Fayette. In the *Almanach royal* for 1790, p. 428, they so appear, without Christian names given, but each with the street address, "rue de Bourbon." The former was Louis Romeuf, who in 1798 was still in the service of La Fayette, acting as an intermediary between him and Bonaparte (Paul Chanson, *Lafayette et Bonaparte* [Lyons, 1958], pp. 34–35).

[135]Alexandrine Charlotte de Rohan-Chabot (familiarly known as Rosalie), widow of Louis Alexandre, Duc de la Rochefoucauld. Her husband, though a liberal supporter of the Revolution, had been assassinated in Sept. 1792. She was therefore free to marry William Short. However, though the attachment between them was profound and destined to last for nearly fifty years, she was apparently restrained from actually marrying him by an ideal sense of duty toward the aged Duchesse d'Anville, her mother-in-law. Even after the death of the latter in 1798, she still declined to marry him, apparently out of regard for her position as a noblewoman in France (George L. Shackelford, "William Short, Jefferson's Adopted Son" [University of Virginia Dissertation, 1955], *passim*).

[136]William Short (1759–1849), the distinguished American diplomat who had served as Jefferson's private secretary in Paris and then had become secretary of legation. Upon Jefferson's return to America in 1789 he became chargé d'affaires. After serving in several other diplomatic posts, he was again resident in Paris from 1795 to 1802.

[137]Marie Charles César Fay, Comte de Latour-Maubourg (1758– 1831). A colonel in the Army before the Revolution, he was elected a deputy of the Noblesse in the States General. He early took the

We regretted very much Puzy['s][138] and my father's absence and drank their healths.

My hotel being two or three doors only from the Opera,[139] I sometime go in the night to[140] the Masquerade,[141] because I am sure to meet there all my American friends. Though few of them can speak French and they have not many acquaintances, they are all extremely fond[142] of this diversion. The ladies of Paris love[143] strangers above all things and all the little engaging attentions, preferences etc., are always for them.

The young men dress here in the most foolish and ridicu-

---

side of the Third Estate and was a leader in the formation of the National Constituent Assembly. He continued to support the revolutionary cause until the summer of 1792. At that time while serving as *maréchal de camp* in the army of La Fayette, disillusionment overtook him, and he accompanied the latter in his flight on 19 Aug. Arrested by the Austrians, he shared La Fayette's long captivity. The Directory secured his release in 1797 and permitted his return to France. With Bonaparte's favor he became a member of the Legislative Body in 1801 and of the Senate in 1806.

[138]See p. 29, n. 74.

[139]The Opéra at this time was located in the theater which Mlle Montansier had had built on the rue de Richelieu opposite the Bibliothèque Nationale, and which had been taken over by the state and made national property in 1794. Victor was then living in the Hôtel de Paris on the rue de Richelieu, only a few doors away.

[140]MS *of.*

[141]The reference would seem to be to the somewhat notorious Bals de l'Opéra (often bals masqués) which were held at the Opéra in the eighteenth century. In an account of them dating from the 1760's, they are said to have begun at 11 o'clock at night and ended at 7 o'clock in the morning, with an admission charge of six livres (*État ou tableau de la ville de Paris* ..., nouvelle éd. [Paris, 1761], pt. III, pp. 12–13). In Victor's Day Book, Expences, under 28 Feb. this item appears: "Bal at the Opera 12 livres." In a later passage (pp. 53–54) Victor compares these Bals de l'Opéra with the less crowded masquerades that were being given in the locale of the rising new theater on the rue Chantereine, renamed "rue de la Victoire since Bonaparte had lived in it."

[142]MS *found.*   [143]MS *loves.*

lous manner; nothing is the *ton* but English fashions. However, their way of copying them is so extremely *outré* that
they make themselves complete *Caricatures*. Their breeches
are very large and the waistband goes up to the Cravat; the
waistcoat is not more than 6 inches long; the Cravat covers
the nose, and they always take it down to speak. The hair,
cropt very short behind, covers the eyes and cheecks. They
wear their watches hanging round their necks with a chain
and placed in a small pocket inside the waistcoat. The coats,
very large before, have no skirts at all or at least they are
so narrow and so short that they do not come half way down
the thigh. So much for a Parisian beau.

MARCH

The 1st of March—I dined with Mr. J. J. Rousseau[1] where
I met old Mr. du Pont, the banker.[2] I soon found there that
all the wise ladies did not live[3] in Rouen; the men of this
family appear to be kept in good nice order and I suppose
at the real standard of their own value.[4]

The 3rd I dined with Mr. Brousse,[5] the 4th with Mr.
de Crillon[6] and the 5th with Regnault de St. Jean d'Angely.[7]

---

[1] Jean Joseph Rousseau (1748–1837), a Paris merchant or banker
who in 1799 was listed by du Pont de Nemours as a subscriber in
the amount of 10,600 francs to the projected Du Pont de Nemours,
Père et Fils & Cie (*Life of E. I. du Pont*, V, 103). His role during the
Revolution was that of a moderate.

[2] Jean Dupont (1736–1819), merchant and, later, Paris banker who
amassed a considerable fortune before the Revolution. He fell under
suspicion and was imprisoned during the Terror, but escaped death
and was released after the fall of Robespierre. He rose to favor under
Napoleon and was made a count and senator and, finally, under the
restored monarchy, a peer of the realm.

[3] MS *leave*.   [4] Cf. pp. 20–21.   [5] See p. 32, n. 88.

[6] He is pretty certainly to be identified with François Félix Dorothée
Balbe de Crillon (1748–1820), who in Paris, 22 March 1800, gave a
power of attorney to du Pont de Nemours, then resident in New

Regnault supports his dignity of Counsellor of State with
a great deal of good grace, and grows very fat under his

York, to act for him in negotiations with a Philadelphia merchant
named Homassel (Crillon's power of attorney to du Pont de Nemours,
1 Germinal viii, Longwood MSS). Beginning as a liberal deputy of
the Noblesse in the States General, he was a moderate supporter of
the Revolution until it turned to violence and overthrew the monarchy.
He returned to public life and became a peer in 1815 after the
restoration of the monarchy. In 1799 he appeared as an unsatisfactory
stockholder in Du Pont de Nemours, Père et Fils & Cie, who offered
"us paper on a bankrupt." In 1808 he was listed as the holder of one
and one-half shares of the company, and du Pont de Nemours was
proposing to buy him out since he had never paid in full. Actually
he was paid 5,000 francs, and a debt to him was incurred which was
still troubling the du Pont family as late as 1817 (*Life of E. I. du
Pont, passim*).

[7]Michel Louis Étienne Regnault de St. Jean d'Angély (1762–1819).
A politician in the States General who began as a representative of
the Third Estate and a moderate supporter of the Revolution, he was
imprisoned during the Terror, released after the fall of Robespierre,
and attached himself to the fortunes of Bonaparte from 1796 onward.
He was made a member of the Council of State and thereafter went
on to the enjoyment of many honors and emoluments under the
Emperor. Upon the fall of Napoleon he was exiled and was only
able to return to France with the general amnesty of 1819, shortly
before his death. The author's characterization of him appears to
have been eminently just.

The du Ponts had vainly hoped that he would subscribe and pay
for two shares of Du Pont de Nemours, Père et Fils & Cie, and later
that he would take stock in the powder company. In a memorandum
for Bureaux de Pusy, returning to France in 1801 while Victor du
Pont was still abroad, E. I. du Pont says: "Regnault St. Jean d'Angély
promised me that he would take a share in the powder (that is to say
three shares) but he afterwards told me that it was impossible—
giving his reason. That reason no longer exists, and it would be well
to speak to him again of our desire that business relations should be
established between him and us.... Regnault's business relations and
his knowledge of the subject may be very useful to us and he will
help the more willingly in order to make us forget that he promised
to help with money and did not do so" (*Life of E. I. du Pont*, V, 246;
see also *ibid.*, pp. 101, 104, 164).

embroide[re]d Coat. His wife is as handsome, as precious, as affected as ever; his house [is] furnish'd in the newest style, and they enjoy life and fortune in the best manner. They are just return'd from a voyage in the Low Countries, where he had been sent with a mission from the government. These kind[s] of missions are generally given to Counsellors[8] who have credit and influence, as a particular reward; for according to the practices of the present time, these voyages are always very profitable. Regnault is not without a very good Credit at Court, and one of the *travailleurs*[9] in the Council. The importance of his new station has not, as [it has] many others, rendered him forgetful of his old friends. And if he has not in his nature the power to wish for any thing with any firmness and perseverance, at least all the will he can command is at their service.

The 6th—I was receiv'd [as] a member of the American Club. About 30 of the Americans now in Paris dine together 3 times a month at one of the Restaurateurs of the Palais Royal. The din[n]er is dressed quite in the American style; and there are[10] rules observed, as in these societies in America, where we fancy ourselves transported for a few hours and to our great satisfaction.

The 8th—I went with Harmand and Irenée to dine at Sev[r]es[11] with Mr. Bro[n]gn[i]art, director of the China manufactory.[12] This establishment is very much fallen. It was supported at great expence by the Government which[13]

---

[8]The word *past* seems to have been written before *Counsellors*, and then struck out.

[9]Workers.   [10]MS *is*.

[11]On the Seine below Paris, arrondissement of Versailles.

[12]Alexandre Brongniart (1770–1847), the distinguished French geologist, mineralogist, and chemist, who became director of the Sèvres porcelain factory in 1800. He retained the position until his death, laying the foundations of modern ceramic chemistry and making Sèvres the leading china manufactory of Europe. His *Traité des arts céramiques* (Paris, 1844) is a classic.

[13]MS *who*.

now does not only refuse to advance any money but does not pay punctually [for] what it[14] gets fabricated there for presents. However Bro[n]gn[i]art, who is a very active young man, expect[s] to reestablish soon the credit of the manufactory by making good connections and getting commands from the foreign Countries.

The 9th—I dined with Jurien[15] and met there Forestier[16] and some other[s] of the first Clerks of the Marine Department, Magnitôt,[17] judge of the tribunal of P[r]izes etc. In the evening I went with Mde Magnitot [to] pay my court to the Consul Le Brun.[18] Twice a Decade he receives in the evening all those who are of his acquaintance and have receiv'd Cards of Admission to the Tuileries. These visits are very short. The Ladies only sit[19] down. If you have nothing particular to tell him, or if he does not give you a chance to Speak, you only make your bow. Le Brun is a fine looking man of about sixty—white head and easy manners. All his influence in the Government is confined to finance affairs, and he has very little interest in the appointments. The fact is he has not firmness enough to refuse what is asked from him, and so in promising to every body, he must disappoint a great number. He is suspected of patronising the royalist[s] and emigrants. Cambaceres, in the countrary, is the known

---

[14]MS *he.*

[15]Presumably Charles Marie Jurien (1763–1836), one of the two chiefs of the First Division of the Ministry of Marine (*Almanach national de France,* An x, pp. 114–115). On 10 Aug. 1792 he fought at the Tuileries with the same battalion, *les filles de St. Thomas,* as did du Pont de Nemours. Most of his career was spent in the Ministry of Marine, where after the fall of Napoleon he rose to high office and considerable influence.

[16]One of the two chiefs of the First Division of the Ministry of Marine (*Almanach national de France,* An x, p. 114).

[17]In the *Almanach national de France,* An x, p. 202, he is listed with his address as "C[itoyen] Magnytot, rue de Magdeleine, maison de Lostange." The court of which he was a member is here called *Conseil des Prises.*

[18]See p. 25, n. 51.   [19]MS *sits.*

patron and protector of the Jacobins.[20] His interest is greater with Bonaparte and whoever is supported by him is sure of success.

The 12th, I dined with Hauterive,[21] First Clerk in the Foreign Affairs department, who befriends me very much; and the 13th, I dined with Mrs. Tilden[22] who, in order to make me acquainted with the Minister of Marine with whom I had business, invited me with ·him. La Touche Treville,[23] now [a] great admiral and cousin of Mrs. Tilden, was there also, and some clerks of the Marine—between others Terpan[t],[24] Head Clerk of the Paying Office. I found

---

[20]MS *Jacobines.*

[21]Alexandre Maurice Blanc de Lanautte, Comte d'Hauterive (1754–1830), celebrated diplomat, who was made head of the division of foreign political correspondence in the ministry of Talleyrand (1799) and thereafter functioned as the intimate servant of the government in the preparation of diplomatic documents and in the conduct of foreign policy, not only under Napoleon but under succeeding governments almost until his death. (Frances S. Childs, "Citizen Hauterive's Questions on the United States," Institut Français de Washington, *Bulletin,* 1957, pp. 34–44).

[22]Cf. p. 36, n. 110.

[23]Admiral Louis René Madelène Levassor de la Touche-Tréville (1745–1804). Imprisoned in La Force with du Pont de Nemours during the Terror, he had been released after the fall of Robespierre. Restored to his position in the Navy under the Consulate, he went on to a career of distinction in the naval struggle with Great Britain.

[24]He is variously referred to in correspondence in the Eleutherian Mills Historical Library as "premier commis de fonds à la Marine" (1801), "chef du bureau des fonds à la Marine" (1801), and "chef de la Division des fonds de la Marine." In the *Almanach national,* An x, p. 115, he is listed as "C[itoyen] Terpant, Chef" [of the Third Division of the Ministry of Marine]. His duties are spelled out in considerable detail. The du Pont interest in him appears in a letter to him from Victor du Pont, dated 28 July [1801]: "Je supplie le C'n Terpan de vouloir bien m'accorder un rendezvous. J'ai à lui faire part de diverses propositions faites à notre maison de New York par le Commissaire général Pichon pour le service de la marine aux États Unis" (V. du P. to Terpant, 28 July [1801], Letter Book—1801, p. 30, Winterthur MSS).

Forfait,[25] the Minister, a plain good man with a more than common share of understanding and many great views and good intentions, but intirely bar[r]ed in his undertakings by the wretched situation of the finances.

It was about this time that I made with Harry Grant[26] a speculation by which we were to make a million of Livres apiece. He was to advance the necessary funds and I to get a permit from the Government for the exportation of a million worth of rags. Rags are now worth in France 15 livres the Cwt and in England from 60 livres to 63 livres. I made a very good and short memorial asking the permit for America; and I should have certainly succeeded, by giving away one million to those who would have procured the permit, without the unfortunate occurence of Bonaparte having been lately put very much out of humour by the demand of the renewal of such a permit which had been granted to General L'Asne[27] for the exportation of grain. He said that as all the people [a]round him had no bounds to their Cupidity, he would refuse his consent forever to all such practises.

Bonaparte's only passions are power and Glory.[28] He is not covetous or avaricious and hates pillage and Corruption; and nevertheless his administration will be nearly as badly famed for mismanadgement of finances and money transactions as[29] the reign of the Directory. The Cause of this is chiefly owing to the bad character of those who surround him, especially a quantity of general officers whose only

---

[25]MS *Forfaix*. Pierre Alexandre Laurent Forfait (1752–1807), a marine engineer and designer of ships who became Minister of Marine soon after the rise of Bonaparte to power in 1799.

[26]See p. 38, n. 120.

[27]Probably the famous General Jean Lannes (1769–1809), later Duc de Montebello. In 1801 he was commander-in-chief of the Consular Guard.

[28]The word *Fame* has been struck out here and *Glory* written over it above the line.

[29]MS *than*.

element is[30] plunder. These[31] people have been very useful to Bonaparte in putting him on the throne. They are chiefly Jacobins and could raise factions against him, so long as his power will not be consolidated enough[32] to put him above the reach of their resentment. He is forced to let them have their own way in many things. Besides that, it is said that he looks on this system of venality as a temporary thing and the repressing of it as a drudgery of administration below his notice. His main object now is peace and every thing short of that [is] not to be considered. But he may find himself mistaken in thinking that one may administrate long without any order in the finances, and the deficit, which made the Revolution, which made him a king, is already hanging over him and increasing every day in a dreadfull manner.

Saturday 14th—I dined with Duquesnoy[33] who is now very rich and living *à la mode du jour,* that is at a very great expence. There is not a more active man than he;[34] he is mayor of one of the sections of Paris, Director general of the salt pits; he belongs to all the Commissions for the administrations of the hospitals and establishments for the poors and he finds time to write pamphlets and translate books. He is very much attached to our family.

---

[30]Several illegible letters have been struck out following *is.*

[31]MS *this.*

[32]A word of four letters has been inked out after *enough.*

[33]Adrien Cyprien Duquesnoy (1759–1808). A fellow member, along with du Pont de Nemours, of the States General and the Constituent Assembly, he pursued an increasingly moderate course in support of the Revolution, until in 1794 he was imprisoned along with du Pont in La Force. He escaped with his life only as a result of the collapse of the Terror. A warm friendship developed between him and du Pont during their imprisonment, and later he became an investor in the powder mill of E. I. du Pont and in Du Pont de Nemours, Père et Fils & Cie (*Life of E. I. du Pont, passim*). He enjoyed the favor of Bonaparte from the beginning of the Consulate until 1805, when he was dismissed from office.

[34]MS *him.*

The 15th—I dined at my friend Goold['s][35] of New York and in the evening went to a ball at Mr. Tochon['s],[36] a son-in-law to Mr. Gregoire Homberg of Havre.[37] He was a poor Officer from Savoy, being lodged at the house of Mr. Homberg when his regiment was garrisoned at Havre.[38] He had the good fortune to please the little heiress who is as ugly as any in the family but a great prise for a *Savoyard*.

The 18th—I dined at Beauvillier['s][39] in company with Mr. Constable[40] of New York and Joseph Smith[41] of Charles-

---

[35]Not otherwise identified. The New York City directory for 1801 (Longworth's *American Almanac, New York Register and City Directory for the 26th Year of American Independence* [New York, 1801], p. 178) lists only Edward Goold, living at 37 Wall St. It also lists Edward Goold and Son, counting house, 39 Wall St. Edward Goold had a son, Charles David Goold, born in 1774 (Walter Barrett [*pseud.*], *Old Merchants of New York City* [New York, 1885], IV, 111); but whether either of these Goolds was Victor du Pont's friend in Paris in 1801 is unknown.

[36]He is perhaps to be identified with Joseph François Tochon (1772–1820), born at the Château de Mez near Annecy in Savoy, who found himself forced into the French Army in 1792 upon the annexation of Savoy to France. He had risen to the rank of captain by 1797, when he was able to quit the Army and devote himself to a life of scholarship and publication in numismatics.

[37]See p. 17, n. 22.

[38]MS *Haver*.

[39]The well-known restaurant on the passage Beauvilliers in the area of the Palais-Royal, established in 1790 by the former chef of the Prince de Condé (Edmond Biré, *The Diary of a Citizen of Paris during the Terror,* tr. and ed. John de Villiers [London, 1896], II, 333–334). This was Victor's almost habitual dining place after his return to Paris from Spain.

[40]Presumably William Constable, of New York, a wealthy merchant, shipowner, and speculator in American frontier lands (T. W. Clarke, *Émigrés in the Wilderness* [New York, 1941], pp. 26–30). He was closely associated in business transactions with, among others, Robert Morris and Gouverneur Morris and was in almost daily intercourse with the latter in Paris during a considerable part of 1792 (Beatrix C. Davenport, ed., *A Diary of the French Revolution by Gouverneur Morris, 1752–1816* [Boston, 1939], *passim*). Victor du Pont met him

ton. This restaurateur is one of the best in Paris and has been adopted by the Americans. I was sure when not invited to dine out, to meet there some of my friends with whom I did mess occasionally. In the evening there was a most brilliant Concert at the Opera for the benefit of Mde Grassini.[42] Harry Grant[43] had a box and gave me a ticket. These concerts given now and then for the benefit of some of the first artist[s] are always very crowded and exhibit the greatest show of Parisian luxury. All the places are double price and are all taken one month before hand. It was a great sight, the front seat[s] of the boxes being all full by ladies dress'd in the most magnificent manner. Nothing is so expensive as[44] the dress of the Parisian ladies; they wear Lace's gowns and veils, and the veils only, cost from 70 to 100 louis.[45]

Saturday the 21st—I was invited to[46] Melvill[e's] and found there a large Company, chiefly Americans. Th[omas] Melvill[e][47] is a young man from Boston, who has very much improved by a French education the natural good parts he

---

again in Bordeaux in May 1801 and sent a letter to his wife by him; Constable was then about to sail for New York on the *Argus*.

[41]Joseph Allen Smith, concerning whom the author gives further information, pp. 56–58.

[42]MS *Grassiny*. See p. 26, n. 54.

[43]See p. 38, n. 120.   [44]MS *than*.

[45]A gold coin worth 24 livres.   [46]MS *at*.

[47]Major Thomas Melville, Jr. (1776–1845), uncle of the more famous Herman Melville. The eldest child of Major Thomas Melville, of Boston, a patriot who had participated as an "Indian" in the Boston Tea Party, he had been sent to France about 1793 at the age of seventeen. There he became a highly successful banker and married a French woman. But reverses overtook him and he returned to Boston in 1811. In the War of 1812 he received appointment as commissary with the rank of major. Unable to regain his fortune, he became a simple farmer in Pittsfield, Mass. Monetary troubles pursued him, and at one time he went to jail for unpaid debts. Later he moved to Galena, Ill., where he ended his days in very humble circumstances (correspondence with Professor Wilson Heflin, U.S. Naval Academy, Annapolis).

brought with him [a] few years ago. He was patronised by Perregaux,[48] the banker, who gave him a credit; and he has work'd the same so successfully that[49] he appears to be worth now great deal of money. He has a fine hotel, a coumpting house as elegant as any Banker in Paris, and is certainly the first American house there; and does the greatest part of his countrymen's business.

In the evening there were[50] great illuminations for the Peace;[51] but the weather was so bad that, as the carriages were not allow'd to run, I only went to see the Tuileries, which were exactly what I had seen on former occasions.

The 22d I dined with Alexander[52] of Baltimore and the 23[d], in Company with Gib[b]s[53] from New Port[54] and Mrs. Fenwick,[55] at Leda['s,[56] the] restaurateur. Gib[b]s is an ami-

---

[48]Alphonse Claude Charles Perrégaux (*ca.* 1750–1808), a distinguished Paris banker of Swiss origin. He supported the moderate Revolution, escaped death during the Terror, and was made a senator under the Consulate and finally a count of the Empire.

[49]MS *than.*   [50]MS *was.*

[51]The Peace of Lunéville, concluded 9 Feb. 1801.

[52]Not otherwise identified. The Baltimore city directory for 1799 lists Henry Alexander, a broker, on Commerce St.

[53]George Gibbs (1776–1833), the distinguished mineralogist and benefactor of Yale University, son of George Gibbs, Sr., merchant prince of Newport.

[54]The word *Boston* has been struck out and *New Port* written after it.

[55]Mrs. Joseph Fenwick (née Elenoire Menoir, or Ménoire, of Bordeaux). Her husband served as American consul at Bordeaux from 1790 through 1798 and continued in business in France for some years afterward. A member of a well-known Maryland family "who had been bred in the commercial line," he formed, in association with his brother, Capt. James Fenwick, and with George Mason's son John, the very successful trading firm of Fenwick, Mason & Co. in Bordeaux (George Mason to George Washington, 19 June 1789, Applications for office under Washington, vol. XI, Records of the Dept. of State, National Archives; "Fenwick Record Book," supplied by Mr. Charles E. Fenwick, President, St. Mary's County Historical Society, Leonardtown, Md.). On Mrs. Fenwick see also pp. 64–65.

[56]One of the famous restaurants of the day, located at the corner

able young man who has travelled much. Being very rich,
he lives here in a great style. Mrs. Fenwick is one of the most
extraordinary characters; full of life, wit, and sport, she is
an excellent companion. *Honni*[57] *soit qui mal y pense* is her
motto. She has given up long ago all claims to the reputation
of a prudent woman; and certainly she is far superior to her
reputation, which is much more than many ladies from Paris
can say for themselves. The daughter of Leda is very pretty.
One of the young men who dines there said one day *Que
Mlle Leda est belle, je voudrais bien qu'elle me fit signe*—
CIGNE.[58] The Puns or Calembours[59] have never been so much
the fashion as they are now. You are pestered wit[h] them.
I note this as one of the best I have heard.

The 24th was one of Mr. Biderman[n]'s[60] days.

The 25—I spent the day at Mr. Tochon's[61] country seat at
Boulogne.[62] He is very fond of botanic[s] and has a garden
full of exotic plants. He made me promise him some seeds
from America.

There is a new theatre in Paris which is the handsomest
and prettiest that ever was built. It is situated rue Chantereine, call'd rue de la Victoire since Bonaparte had lived in
it.[63] They expect a company of Italian[64] buffoons to open it;
and in the mean time they give masquerades in the local[e].[65]

---

of the rue Sainte Anne and the rue Neuve des Petits Champs (Biré,
Diary of a Citizen of Paris during the Terror, II, 334).

[57]MS *honny.*

[58]*Cigne,* a swan; according to Greek legend, Leda, the wife of
Tyndareus, was loved by Zeus in the guise of a swan.

[59]MS *Calembourgs.*   [60]See p. 24, n. 47.   [61]See p. 50, n. 36.

[62]Boulogne-sur-Seine, to the west of Paris. From it the Bois de
Boulogne takes its name.

[63]The Théâtre Olympique. This was one of the promotions of Mlle
Montansier. The formal opening took place, 1 May 1801, with the
presentation of *Furberia e puntiglio.*

[64]MS *italians.*

[65]The author first wrote simply *in it,* then crossed this out and
substituted the more formal phrase.

These balls are superior to those of the Opera; they are not so much crowded and have a greater majority of genteel people. I found here one night more than 25 ladies who spoke good English and attacked us in that language.

The 26th, I dined at Harmand['s][66] and the 27th at Mr. de Cas[e]aux['s],[67] a late president of the Parliament of Bordeaux,[68] who wish[ed] very much to settle in America.

Every morning I made [it] a practise to call early on all the people I had business with, and very often unsuccessfully, for it is more difficult than it ever was to get admittance to men in public employ.

The 29th—I dined at a Restaurateur with my brothers Irenée and Pelleport;[69] the 30th at Mr. Brousse['s];[70] and the 31st was one of Mr. de Lessert['s] days.[71]

[66]See p. 23, n. 46.

[67]Guillaume Joseph de Caseaux, who served as president of the Parlement de Bordeaux from his appointment in 1785 until its suppression in 1790 (C. B. F. Boscheron des Portes, *Histoire du Parlement de Bordeaux depuis sa création jusqu'à sa suppression, 1451–1790* [Bordeaux, 1877], II, 447).

[68]One of the thirteen parlements, or high courts of justice, under the ancien régime. Their opposition often set considerable limitations on the powers of the monarchy.

[69]One of his wife's half-brothers (*Recueil de filiations, 1610–1910*: *Descendance de Dominique Richard de Clevant* [n.p., 1913], tableau 42).

[70]See p. 32, n. 88.　　　　　　[71]See p. 31, n. 82.

APRIL

The 1st, 2d, and 3d of April were Longchamps days.[1] I went the second day with Joseph Smith[2] and Lord

[1]The annual Holy Week parade of Parisians through the Champs Élysées and the Bois de Boulogne for the purpose of displaying their own finery and viewing that of others.

[2]See p. 51, n. 41.

Wycomb[e][3] in Smith['s] Carriage. It is a fine travelling carriage, English built, with the coachman['s] box shaped as a phaeton's body and hanging on springs. The livery of the servants, the Crest and arms on the carriage, and its peculiar form attracted on us the general attention. But if we did happen to be ourselves worth[y] of notice, on the other hand very few of the people and carriages there appeared so to us. The *nouveaux riches* who display such unbounded luxury in the interior of their houses, do[4] not dare yet to affect the same so much in public, and[5] their equipages are very plain. All the fashions respecting horses and carriages are imitated from the English, but badly imitated; every thing is either *outré and caricature*-like, or wanting of *tout ensemble*. You find the first fault with the riders on horseback and the second with the carriages. When the carriage is built with taste, the horses are bad or the harness heavy or the servants with wrong dresses. We saw handsome ladies driving with grace and skill, handsome phaetons with good horses, jockeis and Grooms in style; but they were dressed with Gauses, flowers, and ribbons, just as for a ball or a concert and when once covered with dust cut the most miserable figure. So we could not find a single instance of perfect *bon goût*. To an eye accustomed[6] to the English nicety in these matters, some glaring want of taste was soon found in the best of those who had pretentions to the admiration of the Parisian world.

Lord Wycomb[e][7] is son to the Marquis of Landsdown. I had known him in America where he travelled in 1791. He is a very sensible well informed man, of very soft man-

---

[3]John, Earl Wycombe (1765–1809), son of the first Marquis of Lansdowne. He succeeded his father in 1805 (see also below).

[4]MS *does*.

[5]The word *all* has been struck out here and *and* written over it above the line.

[6]MS *accostumed*.

[7]See above, n. 3.

ners, and quite a melancholic turn. An unfortunate love[8] with an Italian Lady made him miserable[9] for [a] few years past; and though not much older than me, he is already all grey. The French government gave him leave to travel through France in going to Italy, from whence he is returning now. This favor is owing to the greater mildness and liberality of the present government and perhaps as much[10] to the well known political character of Lord Wycomb[e] who is a strong opposition man.

Joseph Allen Smith[11] is brother to Tom S[mith] of Charleston and to the famous William Smith[12] who was one of the first orators in Congress and is now Minister plenipotentiary in Portugal. His political opinions do[13] not coincide exactly with those of Mr. W[illia]m Smith who is a warm Federalist. He is [a] moderate, and think[s] that America is far yet from that state of corruption and ignorance which renders almost every nation in Europe, especially the large ones, unfit for any other government but strong and despotic ones. I know few men whose ways of thinking are more like mine than J[oseph] Smith['s], and that made my acquaintance with him grow more and more intimate every day.

We were both very much affected at the news of Louisiana being ceded to France by a secret art[icl]e of the treaty which made the Duke of Parma King of Tuscany;[14] and we wrote together a short but strong memorial which was given to Joseph Bonaparte, and in which we demonstrated that the possession of that Colony by France should be the unavoidable Cause of a rupture and of a cruel and everlasting inimity [sic] between her and the United States; and that the

---

[8]A word of three letters has been inked out before *love*.
[9]The word *quite* has been struck out before *miserable*.
[10]The words *and perhaps* have been struck out after *much*.
[11]See p. 51, n. 41.
[12]William Loughton Smith, 1758–1812.
[13]MS *does*.   [14]The Treaty of St. Ildefonso.

true interest and best policy of the Republic, and the greatest Glory of the first Consul, should be to declare Louisiana
independant—the consequence of which step would have
been her joining the confederacy of the United States.[15]
However our eloquence was thrown away. We soon learnt
that Cupidity,[16] that great mover of every thing now in
France, which is to be found in lieu of public spirit, and
which governs yet more firmly[17] than Bonaparte, had made
the possession of that colony quite the hobby horse of all
those who have any influence in the government. Companies
are already formed, which outbid one another with good

---

[15]The text of this memoir, addressed to the foreign minister,
Talleyrand, and actually handed to the French government, has not
come to light, but a rough draft of it much marked up and revised, in
the hand of Victor du Pont, has survived (V. du P. memoir beginning,
"Il paraît certain que l'Espagne a cédé la Louisiane à la France"
[1801], Winterthur MSS). It bears the date "1803" in a later hand,
but the correct date is certainly 1801, before 23 April. In a letter
to his wife on that date, Victor, cautioning her not to mention the
cession of Louisiana if it is not already known in the U.S., gives the
following somewhat different account of the preparation and presentation of the memoir. "J'ai fait un superbe mémoire pour engager le
Gouvernement à la rendre indépendante ou à la céder aux Américains.
Il a été présenté à Joseph Bonaparte par Allen Smith de Charleston,
le frère de William Smith, ministre en Portugal, charmant jeune
homme avec lequel je me suis très lié. Mr. de La Fayette et moi avons
agi de concert dans cette affaire. Cela n'a pas réussi, mais cela me
donnera un grand crédit auprès du Gouvernement Américain, qui
sera instruit de toutes parts de la lance que j'ai rompue en sa faveur;
et ici on ne peut m'en vouloir, car ce projet était présenté comme le
plus avantageux à la France et le plus nuisible à l'Angleterre" (V.
du P. to Mme V. du P., 23 April 1801, Winterthur MSS).

His thinking on this subject goes back to a memoir written in 1787
by Barthélemi Tardiveau, a Frenchman then resident in the U.S.,
and to a report of 1789 by the Comte de Moustier, French minister to
the U.S. (see the draft of a letter by Victor du Pont, presumably to
Joseph Bonaparte in 1801, Winterthur MSS).

[16]The words *which is* have been struck out after *Cupidity*.

[17]A word has been struck out following *firmly*.

will and *douceurs* to the ministers, some for the working of
mines, some for the Cutting of timber, and some even for
the privilege of smuggling goods in[to] New Spain. We con-
forted ourselves with the hope that the general peace might
yet[18] rescue Louisiana from the grasp of the French and
save to America the trouble of quarelling with so powerfull
and so dangerous a neighbour—and more still with the
certainty that our children would see the day when not only
Louisiana but Mexico and Peru[19] would, in spite of Spain,
France, and all Europe, emancipate themselves and take
shelter under the spread wings of the American Eagle.

J[oseph] Smith lives[20] in the faubourg St. Germain where
lodgings are so cheap that he has got the greatest part of an
hotel,[21] which[22] did belong to a farmer general and is still
beautifully furnish'd, for 25 louis a month. There is a garden
of more than three acres with most charming walk[s], thickets
and groves. It is call'd the hotel Dorsay,[23] rue de Varennes.
Whenever I began my morning rides by that part of the
town, I always stop'd to take a good dish of tea with sweat-
meats, a political, philosophical, or sentimental conversation,
an[d] when the weather permitted, a long walk in the garden
with my new friend.

The 4th—I dined with my old friend Swan[24] *tête-à-tête* in
order to talk of some schemes against the Spanish dollars in

[18]The word *should* (?) has been struck out here, and *yet* has been
written over it above the line.

[19]MS *Perou.*   [20]MS *leaves.*
[21]A mansion.   [22]MS *who.*

[23]The Hôtel d'Orsay, 69 rue de Varennes (now Varenne) which
extends from the Hôtel des Invalides southeastward to the boulevard
Raspail.

[24]Doubtless James Swan (1754–1830), American patriot, financier,
speculator, and agent of the French government. Born in Scotland,
he emigrated to Boston in 1765, played an active part in the American
Revolution, rose to some position in Massachusetts politics, speculated
heavily in lands, lost, and went to France in 1787 to recoup his fortune. There he met with success and gained control of the U.S. debt

South America. Swan is sometimes without money but never without some great speculations on foot. He claims here now a balance of two millions due to him by the French Government, and is in a fair way to have not the money but the title, which is not quite the same thing. However, there is no doubt but that his natural ingeniosity will make the best of it. When he first arrived to present his acc[oun]ts he was put in the Temple for 3 months and afterwards ordered out of the country. However the matter was compromised. A man who deals in millions is always sure to find friends in Paris.

The 6th—Warin[25] got me an invitation for a private ball at a Mrs. Soubiran['s], a Dutch lady of great fortune, who was better known to the world under the name of Mde Lescins.[26] She has already killed three husbands, *sans compter les autres*,[27] and is one of the most notorious *Messalina[s]* of the present age. . . .[28] All these little anecdotes[29] do[30] not prevent her receiving the first company in Paris. I met there Generals and their wives,[31] the Batavian Minister[32] and his lady, etc., etc.

---

to France (1795). Another of his successes was the establishment of a manufactory of rum at Passy, near Paris. But misfortune again overtook him, and he spent many years at the end of his life in a debtors' prison in Paris. The identification is made nearly certain by the entry of 9 Sept. in the Addendum below: "Din[n]er at Swan['s], Passy."

[25]Nicolaas Warin, of Amsterdam, who had crossed with him from New York (see p. 6, n. 12).

[26]All efforts to obtain further information about this extraordinary figure have met with failure.

[27]Without counting the others.

[28]The author added particulars in six additional lines, but evidently he, or someone else, thought better of what he had written and obliterated it.

[29]MS *anectodes*.   [30]MS *does*.   [31]MS *wifes*.

[32]The Dutch minister, Count Rutger Jan Schimmelpenninck (1765–1825), Holland at that time having become a French satellite under the title of the Batavian Republic. He later became the Grand Pensionary of the Batavian Republic.

The 8th I dined at Dallarde['s][33] and the 10th we gave a din[n]er on fish at La Rapee[34]—Petit de Villers[35] and me to General Collot,[36] Mess[rs] Homberg,[37] Tochon,[38] etc., with my brother and other friends. The cause of it was the appointment of Collot to the government of Louisiana, and the wish of his protection for some Commercial schemes in that Country.[39]

---

[33]Pierre Gilbert Leroi, Baron d'Allarde (1749–1809), 680 rue des Mathurins, Paris. He had been a colleague of du Pont de Nemours (elected by the Noblesse of Saint-Pierre-le-Moûtier) in the States General and National Constituent Assembly. After the dissolution of the Assembly, he withdrew from politics and devoted himself to business. He had important business relations with the du Ponts: e.g., in 1799 du Pont de Nemours writes to Bureaux de Pusy: "Our colleague d'Allarde has a half-share ... in the ownership of five hundred thousand acres ... [in America]. He has promised me his authorization to sell or administer his property and to put the money into our Company" (Life of E. I. du Pont, IV, 291 et passim).

[34]The quai de la Rapée is located on the right bank of the Seine as it enters Paris from the east. Several popular restaurants were located along it (Edmond and Jules de Goncourt, Histoire de la société française pendant le Directoire [Paris, 1855], pp. 102–103).

[35]See p. 11, n. 38.

[36]Victor Collot (1751–1805). Because of his considerable experience in the New World, he was sent in 1796 by the French minister at Philadelphia to make a reconnaissance survey of the western territory along the Ohio and the Mississippi rivers, which was then engaging the attention of the French government. Later, as Bonaparte's ambition unfolded, he was slated for the governorship of Louisiana. His work on the survey resulted in a book published posthumously as Voyage dans l'Amérique septentrionale (2 vols., atlas; Paris, 1826). See Edward Channing, A History of the United States (New York, 1917), IV, 303.

[37]See p. 17, n. 22.

[38]See p. 50, n. 36.

[39]In a letter to his wife, 23 April 1801, Victor writes somewhat more revealingly as follows: "Si je n'avais tenu si irrésistiblement à cette maison [Du Pont de Nemours, Père et Fils & Cie] qui ne peut marcher sans moi, j'aurais eu une belle chance de fortune. La Louisiane est cédée à la France et le général qui y est nommé m'aurait emmené comme intendant. Il me l'a proposé. Il m'a proposé d'aller y établir

The 11th—I dined at Mr. Le Couteu[l]x Canteleu['s],[10] who is a Senator. He was ruined, as the rest of his family, in the beginning of the Revolution, but he has since bought with assignats[41] such quantity of Abbeys, convents, and other church lands in Belgium[42] which have raised so much in value since the peace that he is worth now more than three millions of livres in landed estates.

About this time my friends and especially Mr. Biderman[n][43] thought I had better go to Madrid. I did like the journey very well on acc[oun]t of pleasure and information; but I had no great opinion of its success respecting our business, knowing that [a] great many were there before me on the same schemes, with at least as good means of success as I could command. However Mr. Biderman[n's] desire[44] was

---

une maison de commerce sous sa protection et avec tous les avantages imaginables. Je n'ai pas rejeté entièrement ce dernier projet. Nous pourrions au moins y envoyer un commis" (V. du P. to Mme V. du P., 23 April 1801, Winterthur MSS).

[40]Jean Barthélemy Lecouteulx de Canteleu (1749–1818). A moderate supporter of the Revolution, he had been a member of the States General and the National Constituent Assembly, devoting his attention very largely to economic and financial affairs. He escaped arrest during the Terror and again served as a moderate in the Council of Ancients under the Directory. An ardent supporter of Bonaparte, he was promptly made a member of the Senate. Upon the fall of Napoleon he was made a peer of France by Louis XVIII.

[41]The paper money of revolutionary France, so called because it was supposed to be issued on the security of the national lands *(biens nationaux)*, i.e., lands of the church which were appropriated by the state in Nov. 1789. After its catastrophic depreciation it was used by successful speculators to acquire national lands at scandalous prices.

[42]MS *Belgic.* The extension of the Revolution into Belgium and the annexation of that territory to France had resulted in confiscation of church lands there also.

[43]See p. 24, n. 47.

[44]The word *wish* has been struck out here and *desire* written over it above the line.

an order for me, and I prepared[45] to go as soon as I should have furnish'd myself with proper letters of introduction and recommendations.

Mr. Johannot[46] entered into a negociation with Mrs. Bacciochi,[47] a sister to Bonaparte, and the favorite of Lucien[48] who is ambassador in Spain and a kind of sovereign there; and I got from her strong letters for her brother and her husband General Bacciochi,[49] who was also in Spain, employed to the army of Portugal.[50] The letters explaining to them the purport and consequences of my business were sent before me by a private extraordinary courrier of Lucien. I had many other letters from Lucien's best friends an[d] even from those who were not his great friends, such as Talleyrand, who is at great variance with him; but for decency and decorum's sake it was necessary I should have my credentials from the minister to the Ambassador. That letter of Talleyrand I will copy here as a specimen of his politeness, or rather to shew that fine words are as cheap here now as they ever were.

---

[45]The word *myself* has been deleted following *prepared*.

[46]See p. 25, n. 50.

[47]Mme Elisa Bacciochi (1777–1820), the eldest sister of Napoleon Bonaparte. In 1797 she married Félix Bacciochi, an impoverished Corsican nobleman, who with Napoleon's favor rose to the high positions of senator and general. In 1805 Napoleon made her the Princess of Lucca and Piombino, where she appears to have ruled with considerable talent, and in 1809 the Grand Duchess of Tuscany.

[48]Lucien Bonaparte (1775–1840), Napoleon's second brother. A member of the Council of Five Hundred in 1799, he played a decisive role in the coup d'état which brought his brother to supreme power as First Consul. As Minister of the Interior he had an active part in the organization of the centralized government at the beginning of the Consulate. Sent as ambassador to Spain to counteract English influence there, he succeeded in drawing Spain into alliance with France in 1801. Later he quarreled with Napoleon and took the side of Pope Pius VII against him.

[49]MS *Bacciochy*.

[50]The French army then making war on Portugal.

THE BIDERMANN FAMILY

Oil portrait, painted *ca.* 1795, showing Jacques André Bidermann (1751–1817), the Paris banker, his wife Gabrielle Aimée Odier (1761–1842), and their three eldest children: Marie Jacqueline, later wife of Adrien du Paty de Clam; Jacques Antoine Bidermann (1790–1865), later known as James Antoine Bidermann, who married Evelina du Pont; and Jacques Franklin Bidermann (1793–1811). The original of this portrait is now owned by M. Jacques-Edmond Bidermann of Paris, great-great-grandson of the banker.

Au Cit[oye]n Lucien Bonaparte.

C[itoye]n Ambassadeur:

Le C[itoye]n V[ictor] du Pont qui a·rempli successive-
ment les fonctions de Commissaire des Relations commer-
ciales à Charleston, de Commissaire général à Philadelphie,
est appelé en Espagne par les affaires d'une maison de
commerce qui lui a confié le soin de ses intérêts. Je vous
invite à lui accorder vos bons offices. Le mérite et les vertus
de son père, les services que lui même a rendus, sont des
titres de recommendation bien propres à lui concilier toute
votre reconnaissance. Bien sur qu'ils ne vous ont pas
échappé, je pourrais me dispenser de les rappeler ici,
si je n'aimais à saisir l'occasion de rendre à cette intéres-
sante famille la justice qui lui est due et de répéter l'opinion
que se sont faite du père et du fils tous ceux qui les ont
connus.

Recevez, etc.

Signé Ch[arles] M[aurice de] Talleyrand

Lucien Bonaparte is one of the most profligate characters
of this age. He has abilities, ambition, and courage, and at
the 18th of Brumaire[51] he displaid more firmness than the
General[52] who turned pale and ready to faint when the
deputies rushed upon him with daggers and turned him out
of the hall. Lucien has the looks of a Conspirator and many
of the qualities innate to it. His great passion is making
money, not by avarice but in order to spend it and satisfy
his numerous caprices, and he is never satisfied. The General
said, speaking of him, that he should die in an hospital,
himself on horseback and their brother Joseph in his bed.

The embassy[53] of Lucien in Spain is a kind of disgrace,
and to get him politely out of the Ministery of the Interior,
where he committed the greatest extorsions. He established
excises and other duties at the entry of every large city in
France and contracted the produce of the same for [a] few
years to companies who paid him privately as *douceurs* from

---

[51]The coup d'état of 18 Brumaire (9 Nov. 1799).
[52]Napoleon Bonaparte.   [53]MS *ambassy.*

300,000 livres to 50,000, according to the size of the city. In that manner the *octroi*[54] of Lyons, which[55] bring[s] 1,350,-000 livres a year, was given for 500,000 to a company which[56] gave him for his good will from 2 to 3 hundred thousand.

Lucien has the ambition of succeeding his brother. He courts the Jacobins who on account of his present services consent to forget the part he plaid on the 18th of Brumaire. It is asserted that a party, at the head of which was Talleyrand and many others, wanted Bonaparte to divorce[57] his present wife, who is too old to get any children, and mar[r]y one of the princesses of some European Court,[58] in order to establish a direct line of succession. The Consul was almost converted to that plan; but Lucien and Fouché,[59] the Minister of Police, opposed it with all their influence. This last makes himself very necessary to his master by new conspiracies which he creates on purpose to get credit of their discovery.

For ten days I was very busy putting my affairs into order, preparing for my journey, and writing to America. Petit de Villers left Paris for Le Havre[60] the 21st. Irenée was not yet ready to go and I was much effrayed would loose the opportunity of the Franklin. I left him in Paris.

I refused all invitations to dine out, my time being too precious. I wanted also to see a little my brother, having had very little of his company till then, as our different pursuit[s] kept us in different circles. I dined at the restaurateur with him, and occasionally with my brother Pelleport,[61] Harmand,[62] Lamotte,[63] Beliard,[64] and some other friends.

I could not however refuse Mrs. Fenwick[65] who insisted

---

[54]The toll or tax on goods entering the city.

[55]MS *who*.   [56]MS *who*.   [57]MS *divorce with*.

[58]MS *courts*.   [59]See p. 15, n. 13.

[60]MS *haver*. Petit de Villers was evidently still functioning as supercargo on the *Benjamin Franklin*.

[61]His wife's half-brother.   [62]See p. 23, n. 46.

[63]See p. 41, n. 132.   [64]See p. 102, n. 3.   [65]See p. 52, n. 55.

upon my giving her one day, as she has many commands for me to carry to Bordeaux to her mother and family; and she was so good also as to join to the list of them an order on her house keeper to take from her cellar[66] as much old Madeira as I would choose to carry with me to Spain. Her brother Menoire,[67] a charming young man officer in the engineers, was then in Paris; and I met there also a Mrs. Isnard[68] from Lyons who possess[es] a fine vineyard[69] on the Rhone and promised to send me some of her best wine in order to find a market for it in America.

Arnault,[70] the Poet and member of the Institute who[m] I meet sometimes at Regnault de St. J[ean] d'Angely['s],[71] is just returned from Madrid. He told me that the only way to travel in Spain with a little confort was to ride post on horseback. There is no stage between Bayonne and Madrid, and the mule *coches de Colleras*[72] are from 15 to 48 days to perform that journey. It was recommended to me to have a faithfull servant, as the roads are not always safe nor the

---

[66]The word *house* (?) has been struck out here and *cellar* written over it above the line.

[67]Alexis Guillaume Ménoire, born 15 July 1776, at Bordeaux (see p. 98, n. 8).

[68]An Isnard, located at Place St. Vincent, Lyons, is listed among the "Marchands Épiciers" in 1804–1805 (Duverneuil and La Tynna, *Almanach du commerce,* An XIII, p. 530).

[69]MS *wineyard.*

[70]Antoine Vincent Arnault (1766–1834), a French dramatist who enjoyed a considerable reputation from 1791 until the fall of Napoleon. An ardent supporter of Bonaparte, he was commissioned to reorganize the government of the Ionian Islands, and was made a member of the Institute and secretary general of the Imperial University in Paris. He remained faithful after the fall of Napoleon and went into exile for a time, but he was permitted to return to France and was restored to his honors after 1819.

[71]See p. 44, n. 7.

[72]MS *mules coachées* or *Collieros.* The *coche de colleras* was a heavy coach drawn by six mules harnessed with collars. For a fine description see Jean François, Baron de Bourgoing, *Travels in Spain* (Dublin, 1790), I, 3.

tavern[s] neither. I have[73] taken to travel with me my old servant Villars[74] who has been several times in Spain and talks the language.

D'Autremont,[75] late secretary of Mr. Talleyrand, had some business in San Sebastián.[76] We agreed to go together in a Post chaise as far as Bayonne, and left Paris Sunday, the 26th, at 5 o'clock in the afternoon. The weather was very fine. The roads are very good in the neighbourhood of Paris. We went all night, Villars running before us as courrier. The next day at a quarter before six o'clock in the afternoon we arriv'd at Tours, and so rode 60 leagues in less than 25 hours. It is one of the best ride[s] I ever made. Our Courrier being a little fatigued, the day having been hot, we staid at Tours, got a bath and a good supper, and started at day light.

The 28th—We dined at Poitiers. We met there Mrs. Bruix,[77] the wife of the A[d]miral, going to join her husband to Rochefort. Her carriage was broke. She travelled with her

---

[73]MS *had.*

[74]From a record at the end of the Day Book, Expences, it appears that Villars was employed as of 1 April 1801 at "400 livres the 1st year and 500 livres the others," of course plus maintenance. Outlays for him appear regularly hereafter in the expense account. Victor kept him throughout the remainder of his sojourn abroad and took him back with him to New York.

[75]Louis Paul D'Autremont (d. after 1833), eldest son of Hubert and Marie (d'Ohet) D'Autremont. He had come to this country with his widowed mother and two brothers in 1792 but returned to France with Talleyrand (whom he had met at Asylum, Pa.) in 1796 (John A. Biles, *Historical Sketches Pertaining to or Linked with Asylum* [Geneva, N.Y., c. 1931], pp. 52, 54). The close friendship between him and Victor du Pont and also business relations between the du Pont and D'Autremont families over a long period are revealed in numerous documents in the Eleutherian Mills Historical Library.

[76]MS *St. Sebastien.*

[77]Wife of Eustache de Bruix (1759–1805), the celebrated admiral who became for a time Minister of Marine under the Directory and was picked by Napoleon to command the fleet of barges with which he hoped to invade England.

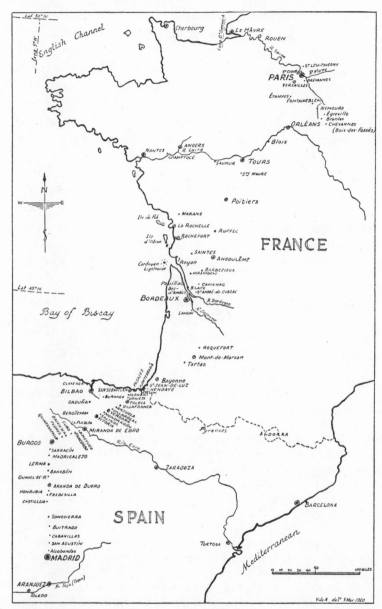

MAP ILLUSTRATING THE AUTHOR'S ITINERARY IN FRANCE AND SPAIN

daughter and chamber-maid and a very handsome young officer to protect her. We went all night and stopped only for din[n]er next day at Barbezieux,[78] at a man famous for the *truffes pyes*[79] he makes in the winter and which are sent to Paris [and] to the first capitals of Europe and even in the West Indies. The maid servant was certainly the daughter of some emigrants of the Vendée[80] reduced to that situation by the Revolution. Though she was not fond[81] of talking in the beginning and would not confess who she was, we soon found that she must have received[82] a most liberal education.

The road grows worse and worse as you approach[83] Bordeaux and would be intolerable[84] was it not for the dryness of the Season. As the ferry over the Dordogne is not to be cross'd in the night, we were obliged to stop in the night at a poor village call'd Cavignac[85] where they asked us 12 livres for an omelette of 12 eggs.

Thursday 30th—We arrived at Bordeaux at 10 o'clock A.M. We found the best hotels intirely full and went to the Hotel de France. This affluence of strangers is owing to the army going into Spain to invade Portugal.[86] Besides the gen-

---

[78]MS *Barbesieux.*

[79]*Patés truffés.* The truffles of this region have been famous since the fifteenth century.

[80]One of the departments of France, situated on the Atlantic in the ancient province of Poitou. It gave its name to the great counter-revolutionary movement which began there in 1793 and was only suppressed after a great struggle in 1795.

[81]MS *found.*

[82]MS *have had received.*

[83]MS *approach from,* a gallicism.

[84]MS *intorelable.*

[85]MS *Cavagnac,* which is clearly an error for Cavignac, department of Gironde, on the main road to Bordeaux, less than 10 miles before it crosses the Dordogne River.

[86]Portugal, in alliance with Great Britain, had declared war on Spain, 10 Feb. 1801. Spain being then in alliance with France, Portuguese territory was promptly invaded by a Franco-Spanish army, and on 6 June Portugal was forced to conclude the Peace of Badajoz.

erals and Commissaries and their numerous retinue, never was an army followed by such [a] quantity of plunderers. They all think that the Conquest and of course[87] the pillage of Portugal will be a very easy thing; and consequently all the adventurers, Gamesters, picaroons, Chevaliers d'industrie[88] from Paris go[89] along in great style. Some call themselves merchants, some contractors; some are acknowledged as 4th or 5th secretaries to the second Secretary of the first secretary of a General or intendant. Their object is to smuggle goods in[to] the country under the protection of the army, sharing the profit with the officers; or to buy from the soldiers their plunder at a cheap rate, especially jewels and diamonds. In fact I cannot compare them but to the[90] swarms of raven[s] that sometimes follow the armies to feed on the corpses.

We were obliged to stay one day to have our Chair[91] and harness mended. I took also some more letters of recommendations from my friends.

---

[87]The word *consequently* has been struck out and *of course* written over it above the line.

[88]Sharpers, men who live by their wits.

[89]MS *goes*.   [90]MS *these*.

[91]The reference is to the post chaise in which they were traveling, the words *chaise* and *chair* having a common origin.

MAY

We left Bordeaux at 6 o'clock A.M., the first of May, and went all night. The roads are very stony in the vicinity of Bord[eau]x and afterwards nothing but sands. That Country is called les Landes; it is a kind of wilderness producing nothing but ferns. Now and then you meet some pine barrens. The only large place you meet is Mont de Marsan, the chief lieu of a department.[1] You travell on very slow.

---

[1]The department of Landes.

The horses are very bad, and the postillons walk on foot almost all the time.

We slept at Tartas Saturday. It is a very romantic old village. Started before day and did not arrive in Bayonne before 4 o'clock in the Sunday afternoon. The taverns were still more crowded here than in Bordeaux; we could not find a room but at a small dark dirty house near the Spanish gate. The peasants in the Landes are a kind of half savages. They wear very strange heavy round woosted[2] caps, much like a Turkish turban.

Monday we staid at Bayonne. The town is pretty and there is a most beautiful walk along the river, with a fine prospect of the citadelle on the other side, and of the vessels anchored in the river.[3] This place does not look so much desolated by the war as[4] Bordeaux. It[5] has kept a constant trade with Spain and much greater since the Americains, who cannot come to France,[6] resort to San Sebastian. There are[7] also several armaments made here under Spanish colours for Vera Cruz and insured at 40%. They are fine fast sailing schooners, and out of three or four there is always one which[8] escapes the English cruisers.

Tuesday 5th—We left Bayonne at 6 o'c[lock] A.M. on little pony horses which carry[9] you to Port Passage[10] in Spain. The roads are intolerable beyond description. At every step

---

[2]I.e., *worsted*.

[3]The Adour River. The quays were along the right bank below the citadel.

[4]MS *than*.   [5]MS *she*.

[6]For several years the U.S., though striving to maintain the position of a neutral in the great struggle between France and Great Britain, had been drawn into a position of virtual war with France, the "Quasi War," as it has sometimes been called.

[7]MS *is*.   [8]MS *who*.   [9]MS *carries*.

[10]Puerto de Pasajes, the landlocked estuary some four miles east of San Sebastián. Travelers had to be ferried across the narrow entrance to the harbor in order to continue on the road to San Sebastián.

we met artillery waggons, broken or overset in holes. They begin to repair these roads for the first time since 10 years, on account of the passage of the King of Etruria,[11] who is expected daily on his way to Paris to thank Bonaparte for his crown. But they only scrape a little the best places, the bad ones would require too much time[12] and too much money; and the turnpike duty which is very high and exactly paid since four years finds many other employ-ment[s].

St. Jean de Luz is a small seaport, intirely ruined; there is not a Boat in the harbour. There is a custom house office where your baggage is[13] examined and pass delivered to you to cross the frontier. I was very much diverted here by an instance of human stupidity; nothing is more ridicule than the air of importance with which men will do the most foolish things under the pretence of executing Laws. There is a Law in France against the exportation of horses. The last place where it should be violated is towards Spain, as the Spanish horses are so much superior to those of this part of France especially. However, no horse can pass without a description of his person, age, sex, color [and] size being entered in full length on the Custom house books—bonds and security being given[14] for his return, pass delivered to him, etc., etc. There are[15] in Bayonne about 12 men, each of whom has[16] 3 or four old ponies with which they carry travel-lers over to Spain: 365 times a year these horses pass[17] St. Jean de Luz, and 365 times all the ceremonies just described are made upon every one of them. The ink, paper, and salary of the Custom house officers employed in that work during

---

[11]Louis, Hereditary Prince of Parma, son of Ferdinand, Duke of Parma. In 1801 by the Treaty of Lunéville the Grand Duchy of Tuscany was taken from Austria by Bonaparte and erected into the Kingdom of Etruria under this prince.

[12]MS *times.*   [13]MS *are.*

[14]The word *entered* has been struck out and *given* written over it above the line.

[15]MS *is.*   [16]MS *have.*   [17]MS *passes.*

the year[18] amount to more than twice the value of the horses.

The village of Hendave[19] has been intirely burnt by the Spanish during the war. Few houses have been rebuilt.

The ferry over the river Bidassoa is the line between the two countries. The famous Isle of Pheasants,[20] known in history by the marriage of Lewis the 14th, is close by the ferry. It is about [a] hundred feet square of mud and nothing else. Over the ferry a Corporal takes your names and a Custom house officer your *pistareens,*[21] or *pesetas.*[22] The road is beautifully kept in order, as the walks of a garden. After you have pass'd the first village call'd Irun,[23] you travel over the mountains and perceive in a fine landscape the town and fort of Fontarabie.[24]

We arrived at Port Passage[25] before sunset. You cross over the bay or harbour in flat boats row'd by women. As soon as

---

[18]The words *amount to more* have been struck out following *year.*

[19]MS *Andaye.* Hendaye is the last point in France along the route before the frontier into Spain is crossed.

[20]Ile des Faisans, in the middle of the river Bidassoa. Here, in a pavilion erected astride the international boundary line, the famous Peace of the Pyrenees (1659) between France and Spain had been concluded. One of its provisions was for the marriage between Louis XIV and the Infanta Maria Theresa, daughter of Philip IV of Spain. In the following June the preliminaries of the marriage were arranged in the same pavilion. "Six long days and the best intentions on both sides were needed to consummate this great affair without offending etiquette. The problem presented was this: How to marry the King of France with the daughter of the King of Spain, without permitting the King of France to put his foot on Spanish territory, nor the King of Spain on that belonging to France, and at the same time not allow the Infanta to quit her father before the ceremony had actually taken place?" (Arvède Barine, *Louis XIV and La Grande Mademoiselle, 1652–1693* [New York and London, 1905], p. 104).

[21]MS *pistoreens.* Pistareen is a word of American or West Indian origin sometimes applied to the old Spanish peseta.

[22]MS *pezetas.*

[23]MS *Iron.*

[24]Fuenterrabía, province of Guipúzcoa.

[25]Pasajes. See p. 70, n. 10.

you arrive in sight of the village where you take these boats,
the women rush upon you, seize the briddle of your horse
and beseech you to give them the preference, and [they]
wont leave you till you have made your choice. Some of them
are pretty and all very neatly dress'd. As I was ahead of my
companions and did not understand well what they said, I
was very much at a loss how to extricate myself of their cries
and hugs. The prospect of this place is most enchanting.[26]
The port is made by a very narrow opening between two
rocks, on the side of which the town is built. It opens in a
circular form all surrounded by hills well covered with
woods. On one of these a co[n]vent of Capuchins adds very
much to the landscape, which is very romantic and appears
to great advantage at the setting of the sun on a warm day.
On the other side of the bay you find other women with
horses to carry you to San Sebastian, distant about one
league. The women carry[27] your baggage on their heads.

You arrive at San Sebastian over an old wooden bridge.
The town is small and built at the foot of a hill covered with
forts and which forms a peninsula. The port is very small
but very good, the citadell very strong, and the general who
took fright at the approach of the French in 1794 and sur-
rendered the town was degraded and confined for life. The
town has suffered very much by the invasion of the French
who have occupied it several months and laid very heavy
contributions. The streets are very narrow.

The 6th—I dined with Mr. Blandin,[28] a French mer-
ch[an]t with whom I had some business. The post road to
Madrid does not pass through San Sebastian, but there is a
Director of posts who delivers you a royal mandate to take

---

[26]The words, *the sea shore is very hilly and,* following *enchanting,*
have been struck out.

[27]MS *carrying.*

[28]Probably to be associated with the firm of Blandin Frères, of
Bordeaux (*Life of E. I. du Pont,* V, 342; VI, 113–114). This firm figures
prominently in the author's Letter Book—1801.

horses at the village of Urnieta[29] which is distant 2 leagues;
but I was very much vexed when I heard from him that for
8 days no private persons could obtain permits, as all the
horses were reserved for the passage of the King of Etruria.
However I found that the *courriers* with official dispatches
were allowed to pass, and I told him that I had several letters
for Mr. Lucien Bonaparte from his family and the Minister
of Foreign Relations which I supposed to be very important.
At the name of Bonaparte every thing was settled: it has
really a magick power all over Spain. It was only agreed that
I should not go the next day, as the King slept at Hernani,
one league this side of Urnieta.[30]

The 7th—The whole city of San Sebastian except [a] few
old women went to Hernani to a fete given to the King. I
sacrificed the curiosity of se[e]ing this little offspring of the
great Republic of France to the pleasure of spending the day
with Mr. Zuaznavar,[31] Director of the Philippines[32] Company,[33] a man of great knowledge and very liberal sentiments. He is a nephew to the famous Marquis d'Iranda,[34]

---

[29]MS *Urnienta.*

[30]MS *Urnienta.*

[31]MS *Zuasnabar.* He is perhaps to be identified with José Maria
Zuaznavar y Francia, a Spanish historian who died about 1840 after
a distinguished public career, a considerable part of which was spent
in San Sebastián.

[32]MS *Phillipins.*

[33]La Compañía de Filipinas, a privileged trading company which
from 1785 to about 1834 enjoyed a monopoly of the trade of Spanish
South America and the Philippines (*The Cyclopaedia; or, Universal
Dictionary of Arts, Sciences and Literature,* ed. Abraham Rees [Phila-
delphia, 1810–24], under "Philippines, Company of the"; Jacques
Peuchet, *Dictionnaire universel de la géographie commerçante* [Paris,
1799–1800], III, 786–790).

[34]Simon de Arragorry, created Marqués de Iranda (or Yranda) by
King Charles III in 1769. A banker or financier of great wealth, he
played an important role in co-operation with the Spanish minister,
Floridablanca, by advancing money secretly to aid the American
cause against England in 1780 and 1781, while John Jay and William

and will share a part of the immense fortune left by that respectable man, dead [a] few weeks ago. The news of that loss was very afflicting for me, as I depended on him more than on any body else for the succes[s] of my operations in Madrid; and [I] had besides some private business with him.

The 8th—In the morning I left San Sebastian on hired horses. We pass'd through Hernani[35] [a] few minutes after the King's departure. The streets were yet covered with flowers. At the post of Urnieta[36] I met with a great difficulty. I had two portmanteaux and thought my servant would carry one on his horse and the postillon the other; but they would not permit it, and insisted upon giving me another postillon. That I would not consent to— on account of the expence, and really it was impossible as, for fear of the robbers, I had not taken more money than[37] was just necessary to reach Madrid. I did reason, swear, expostulate, threaten, all to no purpose. The coolness of the Spaniard was as great as my impatience not to speak well enough to give way to my anger. It would have lost one day to go or send to the Director of the posts at San Sebastian, and I had already lost much time on the road; so I gave up the point and left half of my baggage at the post, not very sure to find it at my return, as they would give me no receipt for it under pretence they didn't know how to write.

Next post is Tolosa,[38] a small town where I stopped to Breakfast. It is 3 leagues from Urnieta[39] and about 5½

Carmichael were in Madrid and Franklin was in Paris. In a letter by Jay to Franklin (Madrid, 21 Feb. 1781), he is characterized as follows: "He is a man of business, abilities, and observation (and what is of much importance here) of money. He keeps the most, and indeed the only, hospitable house here, and persons of the first rank and fashion are found at his table. His consequence at court is unequal to his desires, and, I think, to his capacity of being useful" (Edward E. Hale and Edward E. Hale, Jr., eds. *Franklin in France from Original Documents* [Boston, 1887], p. 422).

[35]MS *Hernany.*   [36]MS *Urnienta.*
[37]MS *but.*   [38]MS *Toloza.*   [39]MS *Urnienta.*

French leagues. The Spanish league[40] is 3600 toises.[41] The post horses are paid so much a league. It comes about to the French price,[42] and you give the driver what you please— nothing at all if not satisfied. The account is pretty difficult as they reckon in *reales de vellón*[43] which is not a *real* money but an *ideal* one.

The altercation in the morning had put me out of spirits with the journey, the inhabitants, and the country; but the superb roads, excellent horses, fine looking people, good wine, and a romantic country did soon recall my good humour. The post horses are large stallions but gentle, easy, and swift. This part of Spain does not look more like the interior of it than[44] the country around Paris like[45] the barren lands[46] between Bordeaux and Bayonne. The three provinces of Guipúzcoa,[47] Álava,[48] and Biscay,[49] and especially the last, have great privileges of which they are extremely jealous. The king cannot lay any taxes without the consent of the representatives of the people which are elected in a very democratic manner, and there are[50] many instances of their having refused the tax. This is perhaps now the only Republic existing in Europe, for a Republic can exist with a King, nobles, and priests. There is no country in the world where there are so many noble[51] families as there are in Biscay and these 2 provinces; but they plough the land and work like peasants, and their pride is satisfied with an old

---

[40]MS *leagues*.

[41]An ancient French measure of about six feet or 1.949 meters.

[42]MS *prices*.

[43]MS *reals de veillon*. The phrase indicates a money of account.

[44]MS *that*.

[45]MS *to*.

[46]Two words following *lands* are struck out and are quite illegible.

[47]MS *Guiposcoa*.

[48]MS *Avala*.

[49]Spanish *Vizcaya*. The three provinces named constitute the Basque provinces.

[50]MS *is*.   [51]MS *nobles*.

rusty sword hanging in their parlour and a very large coat of arms cut in stone over the door of their houses—which things are not in the least troublesome to their neighbours.[52]

From Tolosa[53] you go through Villafranca,[54] Anzuola,[55] and Villarreal,[56] the road turn[ing] several mountains, following a small river, or rather a torrent, over which there is a quantity of handsome high bridges, some built by the Moors, the road going from one side of the river to the other.[57] Some of these mountains are very romantic.

From Villarreal to Vitoria[58] the country is more level, very fine, and well cultivated and looks like a garden. The roads are[59] most excellent.[60] The fact is that going from France into these provinces you go from the country where liberty has done more harm to the country where liberty has done more good, and the difference is more sensibly felt.

I arrived at Vitoria[61] before night. It is 20 leagues from Urnieta.[62] I staid at the post house where I found a good supper and very clean bed. It is an advantage those who travel[63] on horseback have of the carriages: the inns or

---

[52]The privileges enjoyed by the Basque provinces (which were only welded into the Spanish monarchy by degrees between the twelfth century and the fifteenth or sixteenth) were notorious, and they lasted well into the nineteenth century. By an ancient privilege, said to have arisen from the heroic defense of the territory against the Moors, all natives of the country enjoyed the right of *hidalguia* (gentility). The provinces had their own laws and customs, and decrees of the Cortes, as well as royal ordinances, had no force among them unless accepted by provincial juntas.

[53]MS *Toloza.*

[54]Villafranca de Oria, province of Guipúzcoa.

[55]MS *Azuela.*

[56]MS *Villa real.* Villarreal de Alava.

[57]The road makes its way up the valley of the Deva.

[58]MS *Vittoria.* Vitoria is the capital of the province of Alava.

[59]MS *is.*

[60]The words *a garden* have been written after *excellent* and struck out.

[61]MS *Vittoria.*   [62]MS *Urnienta.*   [63]MS *Travels.*

posadas are detestable, but the post masters who entertain[64] no body but courriers are generally rich and keep comfortable houses.

The town was full of French troops. Louis Bonaparte was there with his regiment of Dragoons which is a superb regiment. This is a very young brother of the Consul. He affects to be very fond[65] of a soldier's life and keeps his regiment in fine order. I suppose he has no pretentions of politeness and good breeding; otherwise the nobility of Vitoria[66] could certify the contrary. The greatest honours are paid to him on the road. A great ball was given here, but he laughed at their attentions and turn'd his back upon them. The same complaints are made all along the road.[67] Some of the Generals are great Brutes and they affect to be rude in order to appear Republicans. For example General Desmoulins[68] was lodged at Hernani, in the best house of the place, at a marchioness, sister of the Marquis d'Iranda. In the same house a room was prepared for the King of Etruria who was to arrive the next day. The general upon hearing of this insisted on sleeping in that very room, swearing that no king on earth should fare better than he.[69] He got drunk, abused the ladies, spoiled their furniture, and after all had the room; and the king the apologies of the desolated marchioness. Certainly Bonaparte could not excuse or tolerate

---

[64]A word has been struck out here, and *entertain* has been written over it above the line.

[65]MS *found.*

[66]MS *Vittoria.*

[67]Following this sentence almost three full lines are struck out and are completely illegible.

[68]No general of this name has been identified in the period. It seems not improbable that the author by some misunderstanding has written *Desmoulins* for *Dumoulin,* i.e., Charles, Comte Dumoulin (1768–1847), regarding whom see Six, *Dictionnaire biographique des généraux & amiraux français.* This identification is, however, not certain.

[69]MS *him.*

such behaviour, but no body would dare to mention it to him because it would be putting him in a desagreable situation. Desmoulins is one of the bull dogs who was most active in cleaning the stables of St. Cloud on the 18th of Brumaire.[70]

Nothing is so unpopular in Spain as[71] this expedition against Portugal, which is a Catholic country governed by a daughter of their king, going to be destroyed by the a[s]sistance of French infidels. To the[72] discourses of the priests the conduct of the French troops give new force, so when the peasants can find a soldier or two alone in the country they stabb them instantly; but on the other hand they affect publicly to treat them with regard, friendship, and cordiality. There is only one thing in human nature that can be greater than the hatred and abhorrence the Spaniards keep[73] for the French now—it is the fear they have of them.

Vitoria[74] is the Capital of the province [of] Alava, and pretty considerable for its trade and the number of its inhabitants. I left it next day at daybreak. There is 5½ leagues to Miranda town[75] on the river Ebro which is the limits of the Old Castilla. There is here a custom house, very severe, and the officers will throw the snuff out of your box or the ciggars out of your pocket if you do not secure their good will by a piece of 20 pence.[76] Fortunately for a traveller these *officials del Rey* can be bought at a very cheap rate, otherwise they should be a very great plague. I breakfasted at S[an]t[a] María del Cubo,[77] a small village 5 leagues from

---

[70]See p. 37, n. 115.   [71]MS *that*.   [72]MS *these*.
[73]MS *keeps*.   [74]MS *Vittoria*.
[75]Miranda de Ebro, province of Burgos.

[76]MS *pences*. The English word seems strange here. Can it be that the author was referring to the livre of 20 sous? In his Company Expense Account (which he kept in livres tournois) he records, under date of 9 May at Miranda, "Custom house officers 2 [livres]."

[77]This village has not been identified, though it must have been close to Cubo de Bureba, which was on Victor's route.

Miranda where I found a company of very genteel monks travelling on mules from Salamanca. One of them could speak French and the other English. I drank their health and saluted them very politely. This behaviour quite won their confidence and we had a long conversation upon politics, and other topics. I told them I found their country very good, much better than I expected: we parted very good friends and shaking hands. One of them told me very earnestly, *No indeed you are not a Frenchman.* This reminded me of a compliment I receiv'd in New York sometimes after my first arrival in America: *Indeed you are to[o] good a fellow to be a Frenchman.*

One of the reasons why the roads should be so excellent in this country is that very few carriages are used. All the trade is carried on by mules; you meet very often hundreds of them. They are tied head to tail, fifteen or twenty together, each string or colomn having a driver who sits[78] sleeping across over the baggage of one of them. The last of the band carries[79] a kind of bell or[80] brass drum hanging on her side which you can hear one half league distant. It is a very tedious melancholic noise, which however chears up the mules and serves to warn the Custom houses officers. Heavy penalties are laid on the drivers found without these[81] instrument[s].

Near the village of Pancorbo[82] 2 leagues before Cubo are some tremendous rocks through which the road passes. This place was famous for robbers and a little fort has been built there to keep a guard against them.

I arriv'd at Burgos at 4 o'clock having rode that day 23 Spanish leagues. Burgos is a very large town, Capital of the Old Castilla[83] and situated on the river Arlanzón.[84] Though a little fatigued as the day had been rainy and disagreable, I went immediately to see the cathedral which is much

---

[78]MS *sets.*   [79]MS *carry.*   [80]MS *of.*
[81]Two(?) words, following *these,* have been struck out.
[82]MS *Pancorvo.*   [83]Castilla la Vieja.   [84]MS *Arlancon.*

admired by travellers. It is an old Got[h]ic building, the
exterior not very remarkable but the interior immense and
rich beyond expression. The rails around the choir, nave
and chapels are of brass with tops and other parts gilt, the
altars are astonishingly numerous and all covered with gold
and brilliant stones, and really the whole is most magnificent. There are[85] here, as in every town of Spain, many
co[n]vents, and the number of monks and priests you meet
in the streets is really surprising. There is a square with a[n]
Equestrian statue of Carlos II.[86] The fountains and other
public monuments are fine and there are[87] many antiquities.

I fared very well at the post master of Burgos who is a
pleasant old little fellow. I had a good supper of fresh sal-
mon which they catch in abondance in the river. I begin to
be quite used to the Spanish cookery and even reconciled
to the taste of their oil with which they dress every thing.
This oil is not quite so strong to the taste as the fish oil, but
it has got a rancid smell which evaporates every where and
attachs itself to every thing. If you pass in the street at the
time they cook their din[n]er the flavour of the oil will stick
in your throat; the mules drivers, the mules themselves, their
harness you can smell on the high way half a league to wind-
wards; the houses, the servants maids, the monks, the furniture, every thing which is not cleaned very often—and there
are here many thing[s] in that predicament—do[88] exhale a
strong oily flavour very desagreable to those not used to it.

The country begins to look much poorer and the roads
are not so good on the other side of Burgos.

Sunday the 10th—I breakfasted at Lerma, a small poor
village with four large co[n]vents and a Castle or Country
seat belonging to the Duke of Medinaceli.[89]

---

[85]MS *is.*

[86]Charles II (1661–1700), King of Spain, Naples, and Sicily, successor
of Philip IV, and last of the Spanish Hapsburgs.

[87]MS *is.*   [88]MS *does.*

[89]MS *Medina Coeli.* The reference seems to be the Castle of Lerma,

From Burgos to Lerma 7½ leagues: from Lerma to Aranda[90] 7. This little town looks poor, as well as the inhabitants and the neighbouring country. The roads and post horses are about here nearly as bad as in France; the country is in some places intirely barren, in other[s] poorly cultivated, and every where intirely naked. I have rode this morning five or six leagues without se[e]ing a tree or even a shrub.

The Castilians[91] look[92] very much like the Indians of America; they have nearly the same colour of skin, the same long black hair, and have also much of their character and inclinations, being as well as them Dirty, Lazy, Stinking, robbers and proud.

Ten leagues from Aranda[93] between the posts of Castillejo[94] and Somosierra,[95] are some high mountains which separate[96] the Old from the New Castilla.

All the places I went through appeared to me so miserable that I determined on going on all night. I repented it afterwards as the weather was cold and the road so bad in some places that we went on very slow. I had also some uneasiness about the *ladrones*[97] which inhabit these mountains. However we arrived without any accident at Somosierra[98] about 12 o'clock in the night. I would have kept on, but my man Villars was very hungry, as we had taken nothing since breakfast; and the only horses they could give us were just returning to conduct a courrier. So I determined to stay two

---

which was erected in 1614 by Francisco Sandoval y Rojas, first Duke of Lerma, from whom it passed to his son, the Duke of Uceda. The author seems to have been mistaken in reporting it as belonging to the Duke of Medinaceli, whose seat was located some 100 miles to the southeast of Lerma.

[90]MS *Arranda*. Aranda de Duero.

[91]MS *Castillans*.   [92]MS *looks*.   [93]MS *Arranda*.

[94]Castillejo de Mesleón, province of Segovia.

[95]MS *Somossierra*. The town is just north of the Pass of Somosierra, over the northeast spur of the Sierra de Guadarrama.

[96]MS *separates*.   [97]Robbers.   [98]MS *Somossiera*.

or three hours. We ate[99] some Eggs and slept on benches near the fire, I cannot say near the Chimney for they have none. They make [a] fire in the middle of the house, and the roof is open to let in the rain and out the smoke. But I cannot say that it answer[s] very well this last purpose, for every thing inside of the house is blacken'd by the smoke, except the faces of the inhabitants which are naturally so.

The roads are very fine in New Castilla. To Cabanillas[100] 7 leagues; from Somosierra[101] the country is nothing but mountains which now and then offer[102] a pretty landscape. On the top of some you see old watch towers from the time of the Moorish wars. In general the country is poor and dry. From Cabanillas to Madrid 10 leagues. The country is level and naked—no trees, no pastures, some fields of rye badly cultivated, not a villa or country seat around Madrid, few Co[n]vents, poor[103] as the country itself and that's all. I arriv'd at Madrid at 3 o'clock in the afternoon. I was saluted in the suburbs by the cry *Demonio de Francese*[104] uttered by many children as I went along. At the Gate an[105] officer of the Custom house gallops after you.

---

[99]MS *eat.*
[100]Cabanillas de la Sierra, on the direct road to Madrid.
[101]MS *Sommosiera.*
[102]MS *offers.*
[103]MS *poors.*
[104]Perhaps a little corruptly for "Devil of a Frenchman."
[105]The words *custom house* have been struck out after *an.*

Addendum

ADDENDUM[1]

MAY

11—Arrived at Madrid at 4 o'clock. Lodged at the Cross
of Malta.[2] Tea at Mde Humphreys'.[3]
12[4]—Din[n]er with[5] Longuemare[6] and Ronchamps.[7]

---

[1]The text from this point to the end consists of the dated entries
in the *Pocket Remembrancer,* which was described in the Introduction,
pp. xx– xxii above. Supplementary matter in the footnotes has been
added from the other sources already described in the same context.

[2]The Cruz de Malta, the best inn in the city (Charles E. Kany,
Life and Manners in Madrid, 1750–1800 [Berkeley, Calif., 1932], pp.
149, 426).

[3]MS *Humphries.* Ann Frances (Bulkeley) Humphreys, wife of the
U.S. minister plenipotentiary to Spain.

[4]On the page opposite the entries from 12 to 21 May, the author
has set down the following descriptive notes:
"Madrid fine town. Appears small quantity of churches. Walk of
the Prado well attended and beautiful. Angelus. Aranjuez. The finest
gardens in the world. River Tago—small frigates. Very dull and solitary
Court, doing every day the same thing. Old fashion'd carriages. Bull's
fight: two men and about 20 horses killed on the spot to the great
entertainment of People and Court. Pretty good tavern at Aranjuez.
They are intolerable in Madrid, especially for beds and cooks. 2
theathres [*sic*], very good performers, especially for opera comiques.
Bad smell of garlic in the houses which the smoke of segars cannot
intirely take away."

[5]MS *at.*

[6]Not identified. A merchant of Le Havre named Longuemare de

[87]

The Prado. Messrs. Oyarzábal,[8] Dandinot, Bernard, Solary.[9]
13—Aranjuez. Din[n]er with Lucien Bonaparte. Superb
gardens. Queen.[10] Castle.
14—Din[n]er with the Ambassador again.[11] Gardens.
King and Queen. Comedy—a traduction of the Prisoner.[12]
15—Din[n]er at the Tavern Fontana de Oro.[13] Walks.
Queen's garden.

---

la Salle was active in transatlantic shipping in 1794, but no reason
has been found to associate him with Madrid in 1801 (Moreau de St.
Méry, *Voyage aux États-Unis de l'Amérique, 1793–1798*, pp. 16, 39,
101, 105).

[7]Possibly the Mr. Ronchamps who had been introduced to the
American minister, David Humphreys, through a letter (Sept. 1800)
from Governor Thomas McKean, of Pennsylvania, and whose business
in Spain the minister was requested to forward. In a letter of 2 Jan.
1801, the minister, writing to Wm. Willis, the American consul in
Barcelona, describes Ronchamps as "a Frenchman by birth, but who
has been a long time established in the U.S.," and "a very well bred
and agreeable person in society" (F. L. Humphreys, *Life and Times
of David Humphreys, Soldier, Statesman, Poet* [New York and London,
1917], II, 278, 282).

[8]MS *Yorzabal*. Juan Batista Oyarzábal, a wealthy sugar planter
of Spanish Santo Domingo who was a relative of the Marquis d'Iranda.
In Sept. 1800 the latter wrote to Du Pont de Nemours, Père et Fils
& Cie of New York to invite them to furnish details of their operations
to Oyarzábal and initiate business relations with him (Marquis
d'Iranda to Du Pont de Nemours, Père et Fils & Cie, 8 Sept. 1800,
Winterthur MSS).

[9]Pierre Daudinot [*sic*] & Cie and Solari & Cie are listed among
bankers and commercial houses of Madrid in 1804–1805 (Duverneuil
and La Tynna, *Almanach du commerce*, An XIII, p. 647). Efforts to
identify Bernard have been unsuccessful.

[10]The notorious María Luisa (1751–1819), wife of King Charles IV.

[11]The reference is to Lucien Bonaparte, who, since Nov. 1800, had
been French ambassador to the court of Madrid.

[12]Evidently *Le prisonnier*, a comic opera by Alexandre Duval,
with music by Dominique Dellamaria (see p. 40, n. 127).

[13]MS *di Oso*. There is a difficulty here which remains unexplained.
The manuscript reading *Fontana di Oso* seems to make no sense.
We have, therefore, revised it to *Fontana de Oro*, the name of a well-

16[14]—Din[n]er with the Ambassador. Bull's fight. Play.

17—Gone to Madrid.[15] Prado. Quantity of carriages. Evening at Mr. Humphreys'.[16]

18—Madrid. Din[n]er at Tavern. Theatre. Good opera and farce. Better performers than at Aranjuez. Cold chilly weather.

---

known Spanish tavern of the epoch. But the Fontana de Oro was in Madrid, not Aranjuez. Can it be that the author has made this entry in the *Pocket Remembrancer* opposite the wrong date?

[14]On 16 May, just before his return to Madrid, du Pont began a letter (no. 8) to his wife which he was to finish on 30 May after his arrival in Bilbao.

He begins by announcing a great business disappointment ("Ma grande affaire n'est pas perdue, mais elle souffrira des lenteurs qui m'effrayent"), but then he turns to a more cheerful subject and says: "Ce lieu-ci est vraiment enchanté. Il n'existe pas dans la nature de plus beaux jardins. Aussi je me promène tout le tem[p]s que je n'écris pas, et comme je ne suis pas grand marcheur de ma nature, je rentre tous les soirs aussi fatigué que si j'avais couru la poste."

But he was far from seeing everything in Spain couleur de rose. Continuing the letter some days later in Bilbao, he says: "Ce pays-ci est le bout du monde; je n'y ai pas vu une gazette française .... La province où je suis à present est belle et curieuse, mais rien n'est abominable comme la Castille, ses habitan[t]s et même Madrid la capitale." In the same vein in the same letter he also remarks: "Je me suis amusé à faire un petit recueil d'observations sur l'Espagne, que je ne puis t'envoyer ni t'extraire, mais que tu liras avec plaisir, car il contient plusieurs choses assez plaisantes" (V. du P. to Mme V. du P, 16 May 1801, Winterthur MSS). These candid pleasantries of which, apparently, he intended to make some use in his journal, and which the reader will recognize in certain passages, he chose to write in French. Fortunately they have survived under the title, "Extraits de mon journal en Espagne." They have been reproduced as an appendix at the end of this volume (see pp. 121–127).

[15]In his Company Expense Account he records his bill (145 livres) at the "fonda de Malta," which is presumably the Cruz de Malta where he had stopped on his first arrival in Madrid.

[16]David Humphreys (1752–1818), then U.S. minister plenipotentiary to the court of Spain.

19—M[adrid]. Play. Same weather, very disagreable. Mr. Oyarzábal.[17]

20—Din[n]er at Mr. Humphreys': great hospitality, not to be found at the Spaniards. Mr. Buckelman of Hamburg.[18]

21—Din[n]er at Mr. Dandinot['s].[19] Assembly of Frenchmen. Their rediculous behaviour. Opera comique very well perf~ med.

22—Rainy disagreable cold weather. Many persons sicks. Colick fatal to strangers.

23—Seen the Palace. Difficulties to get an order for post horses. Evening at Mr. Humphreys'.[20]

24—Din[n]er at J. B. Oyarzábal['s].[21] House of Marquis d'Iranda. Prado.

25—Seen a toilet for the Queen—with Mr. Montgomery of Alicant[e].[22]

26[23]—Left Madrid at 2 o'clock A.M. Slept at Somosierra— 16 leagues ½.

---

[17]MS *Yorzabal*. See p. 88, n. 8.

[18]Not identified. He is presumably the same as Bokelman, who appears below under date of 30 May.

[19]See p. 88, n. 9.   [20]MS *Humphries.*

[21]MS *Yorzabal.* Since this gentleman was a kinsman of the Marquis d'Iranda, it may perhaps be inferred that the dinner took place at the Marquis' house.

[22]John Montgomery, a well-known American merchant of Alicante, whose more famous son, George Washington Montgomery, official translator to the U.S. Legation in Madrid, is credited with laying the foundation of Washington Irving's reputation in Spain.

[23]On the page opposite the entries from 26 to 31 May, the author has set down the following descriptive notes: "On the rocks of the highest mountains you see towns erected from the time of the Moorish Wars. Left the France road at Ameyugo. Fine bridges and fine old castles and co[n]vents. High mountains at Orduña [MS *Ordugna*]. Superb road cut in the rocks. End of the province [of] Alava [MS *Avala*]. Custom house. Biscay romantic and well cultivated. Great inondation of the River of Bilbao. Bridges carried away and the greatest part of the town submerged. Great damages caused to shipping and to the wharfs and public walk. No such inondation since 1762.

BULLFIGHT IN THE PLAZA MAYOR, MADRID

From an anonymous print in the Museo Municipal of Madrid, here reproduced from Pedro Vindel, *Estampas de toros* (Madrid, 1931), Plate ccxl.

27—Breakfast at Honrubia.[24] Slept at Lerma—18 leagues ½.

28—Breakfast at Burgos. Slept at Berguenda—26 leagues. Good tavern.

29—Din[n]er at Orduña. Arrived at Bilbao.[25] Lodged at San Nicholas—12 leagues.

30—Affability of Don Francisco Mazarredo[26] to whom I had been address'd by Bokelman. Tertulia[27] at Doña Adán['s].[28]

31—Procession to see home a Virgin Mary which they had carried to town to stop the inondation. Rainy weather.

Bilbao very neat pretty town, many public embellishments. No poors to be seen there."

[24]MS *Onrubia*. Honrubia de la Cuesta.

[25]The Company Expense Account gives the itinerary from Madrid to Bilbao in considerably more detail, as follows: "May 26th: Post Royal to Alcobendas, [livres] 32–10; P[ost] San Augustín [del Guadalix], 18; P[ost] Cabanillas, 16; P[ost] Buitrago, 21; P[ost] Somosierra, 15. [May] 27th: P[ost] Castillejo, 15; P[ost] Fresnillo, 13–10; P[ost] Honrubia, 16; P[ost] Aranda [de Duero], 15; P[ost] Gumiel de Hizán, 11; P[ost] Bahabon, 11; P[ost] Lerma, 16. [May] 28th: Post to Madrigalejo, 13–10; P[ost] Sarracín, 16; Post to Burgos, 11–10; P[ost] Quintanapalla [MS *Quintinapalla*], 18–10; P[ost] Castil de Peones, 18; P[ost] Briviesca [MS *Bribiesca*], 11; P[ost] Cubo, 16; P[ost] Ameyugo, 13–10; P[ost] Bergüenda, 16–10. [May] 29th: Mules to Orduña [MS *Ordugna*], 25; Mules to Bilbao, 30."

[26]MS *Massarido*. Francisco Mazarredo, a nephew of Admiral José Domingo Mazarredo, was a captain in the Spanish Navy, second in command of the ship *San Juan Nepomuceno,* who was killed in the battle of Trafalgar. The information in this note (and n. 28 below and p. 92, n. 4) was kindly supplied by the U.S. consul at Bilbao, with the assistance of the chief librarian and archivist of the regional government of Vizcaya.

[27]MS *Tertullia*. An evening party characteristic of Spanish society in this period (Kany, *Life and Manners in Madrid, 1750–1800,* ch. x).

[28]The reference may be to the wife of Adán de Yarza, an important personage in Bilbao. Before marriage she was Ramona María de Barbachano. A painting of the couple was made by Goya in 1787, and a photograph of it is preserved in the archives of the Diputación de Vizcaya (see n. 26 above).

Addendum

JUNE

1—Walk at Olaveaga.[1] Port where the vessels remain, 2 miles.[2] Tertulia.[3]

2—Ardanas y Bengoa.[4] Rainy disagreable weather. Tertulia[5] at Mrs. Goos[s]ens.[6] Mr. Schwartzman, Mr. Girard.[7]

3—Left Bilbao at 1 o'clock. Slept at Durango. Singular adventure.

4—Arrived at Vergara[8] in the morning with 4 hours rain. Taken the post to[9] San Sebastian at 7 P.M.[10]

5—Rain all day: D'Autremont,[11] Mr. Gilman of Boston.[12]

---

[1]Olaveaga is a western suburb of Bilbao, within easy walking distance.

[2]The important harbor of Bilbao is even more than two miles down the river Nervión from the city.

[3]MS *Tertullia*.

[4]There was a commercial firm named Ardanaz e Hijo y Bengoa at Bilbao in the early nineteenth century (see p. 91, n. 26). The firm is listed among the principal commercial houses in 1804–1805 (Duverneuil and La Tynna, *Almanach du commerce*, An XIII, p. 634).

[5]MS *Tertullia*.

[6]A Don Enrique Alejo Goossens y Moriarty, whose parents had migrated from Antwerp and Cork, was prior of the Consulate of Bilbao in 1798 and lord mayor of the city in 1804. The author's reference may be to his wife, who in 1801 would have been some eighty years old. His daughter, Doña Magdalena de Goossens y Moriarty, was also a social leader in the city who was known for her beauty and grace (see p. 91, n. 26).

[7]Efforts to identify Mr. Schwartzman and Mr. Girard have been unsuccessful.

[8]MS *Bergara*. From Durango to Vergara they traveled on mules at a cost of 32 livres, as the Company Expense Account reveals.

[9]MS *at*.

[10]The Company Expense Account gives the itinerary from Vergara to San Sebastián more fully: "Post Villarreal [de Urrechu], 13 [livres]; P[ost] Villafranca, 16; P[ost] Tolosa, 15–10; P[ost] Urnieta, 16–10; Post San Sebastián, 14."

[11]Louis Paul D'Autremont, who had traveled with Victor from Paris to Bayonne (see p. 66, n. 75).

[12]In the papers of Isaac Cox Barnet, consular agent of the U.S. at

6—Seen Widow Birmingham & Sons.[13]

7—Visit at Port Passage.[14]

8[15]—Left San Sebastian after din[n]er. Slept at St. Jean de Luz.

9—Arriv'd at Bayonne with D'Autremont. Public walk.

10—Din[n]er at the Tavern. Gilman of Boston.[16] Gabriac.[17]

11—Din[n]er at Mr. Dubroc['s].[18] Seen the principal merchants.

12—Din[n]er at Mr. Meillan['s].[19] Walk in the country. Fine houses.

13—Din[n]er at Mr. Galarte['s].[20] Count de Cabarrús.[21]

Bordeaux, there is a declaration, dated 24 Jan. 1801, by the "undersigned citizens of the U. S. residing in Bordeaux" to the effect that they had examined the ship *William Forrest*, of Philadelphia, and found that the cargo would have to be discharged at Bordeaux, on account of the leaky condition of the vessel. The signers are John B. Dabney of Boston and R. Gilman of Boston (Consular Despatches, Bordeaux, vol. I, Records of the Dept. of State, National Archives).

[13]Not identified but presumably an English mercantile firm.

[14]Pasajes.

[15]On the page of the *Pocket Remembrancer* opposite the entries for 8 and 9 June, Victor has set down the following descriptive note: "The village of Bidart [MS *Bidarte*], 2 leagues from Bayonne, produces a particular kind of women—tall, strong, active, and intelligent."

[16]See p. 92, n. 12.

[17]Not identified.

[18]Not identified, but it may be noted that in 1804–1805 a Dubrocq & Cie was listed among the "Négocian[t]s-Banquiers" of Bayonne (Duverneuil and La Tynna, *Almanach du commerce*, An xiii, p. 456).

[19]Probably Arnaud Jean Meillan (1748–1809), a merchant of Bayonne who had been a member (Girondist) of the Convention and of the Council of Ancients but had retired to private life in 1799. In the long letter of 1 Dec. 1800 by du Pont de Nemours, which Victor and E. I. du Pont carried with them to Jacques Bidermann in Paris, the advice is given that Meillan go to Spain with Victor because of his knowledge of Spanish and of his experience in business dealings in that country (*Life of E. I. du Pont*, V, 187). For the whole career of Meillan see Kuscinski, *Dictionnaire des conventionnels*.

[20]Conceivably to be identified with the Galart at whose country

Addendum

[June

14—Left Bayonne at 1 o'clock in comp[an]y with Mr. Daguerre.[22] Sup[p]er at Tartas. Gone all night.

15—Din[n]er at Roquefort. Slept at Langon.

16—Arrived at Bordeaux 1 o'clock A.M. Lodged at Hotel Franklin.

17—Dined with the Americans.[23] Walk and play—Maison a vendre.[24]

18—Din[n]er with Gros Davilliers & Co.[25] Anthoine.[26] Mr. Bousquet.[27] Cercle des Chartrons.[28] Duclos, Secretary of the Prefecture.[29]

---

house near Bayonne, Meillan, then under proscription, had found a hiding place in 1793 (Arnaud Jean Meillan, *Mémoires de Meillan* [Paris, 1823], p. 161, in *Collection des mémoires relatifs à la Révolution française*).

[21]Presumably François, Comte de Cabarrús (1752–1810), the celebrated financier who was born in Bayonne but spent most of his life in Spain or in the service of the Spanish government. He was the father of the notorious Mme Tallien (see p. 37, n. 113).

[22]Not identified, but it may be noted that in the Company Expense Account we read: "Journey from Bayonne to Bordeaux in D'Autremont's Post-Chaise in account with Mr. Daguerre of Bayonne. My half for Post horses and tavern expences, 176–5"; and that in 1804–1805 a Louis Daguerre and Domin[ique] Daguerre were listed among the merchants of Bayonne (Duverneuil and La Tynna, *Almanach du commerce*, An XIII, p. 456).

[23]Perhaps a club or association of Americans then resident in Bordeaux.

[24]See p. 40, n. 131.

[25]Evidently the Bordeaux branch of the Paris banking firm of the same name which supplied the central office and secretary (M. Roman) for Du Pont de Nemours, Père et Fils & Cie (*Life of E. I. du Pont*, V, 121). In 1804–1805 the Bordeaux firm was listed as Gros Davillier [*sic*] & Cie, 1 rue Daurade (Duverneuil and La Tynna, *Almanach du commerce*, An XIII, pp. 107, 113, 156, 465).

[26]A business agent associated with Gros Davilliers & Cie. Some months later Victor du Pont employed him in the forwarding of goods to the U.S. (V. du P. to Anthoine, 1 Jour Complé., An IX, Letter Book—1801, Winterthur MSS). Anthoine also acted for John Bousquet (Anthoine to V. du P., 17 Nov. 1801, Winterthur MSS).

[27]Presumably John (or Jean) Bousquet, a merchant of Bordeaux, with whom Victor du Pont had had some dealings since 1800. E. I.

19—Din[n]er with Mr. Muller,[30] Camescasse.[31] Small theatre.[32]

20—Din[n]er with Mr. Zuaznavar.[33] Gramont[34] & Co.[35] Theatre Circle.

21—Din[n]er at home. Public gardens. Play—Dido.[36]

22—Taken phisic. Play—Paul and Virginia,[37] Mde S[ain]t Aubin.[38]

---

du Pont was still doing business with him as late as 1825 (*Life of E. I. du Pont*, V, 129–132; XI, 134, 137).

[28]Presumably a club or association of businessmen or merchants, taking its name from the quai des Chartrons on the left bank of the Garonne, one of the most active centers of shipping in Bordeaux.

[29]He is obviously the same person as "C[itoyen] Duclaux, Secrétaire-Général" of the prefecture of Bordeaux, who appears in the *Almanach national*, An x (1802), p. 300.

[30]Not identified, but it may be noted that a J. J. Muller, 11 rue Castillon, was one of the principal merchants of Bordeaux in 1804–1805 (Duverneuil and La Tynna, *Almanach du commerce*, An xiii, p. 466).

[31]Probably the "Camescasse, fils" who appears in the *Almanach national*, An x (1802), p. 300, as one of the twenty-four members of the Conseil Général of the department of the Gironde. A letter from the Chamber of Commerce of Bordeaux describes him as a merchant (négociant) whose place of business was at no. 6, rue du Chapeau Rouge.

[32]MS *theathre*.

[33]MS *Zuasnabar*. Evidently the same person whom he had seen in San Sebastián on his way south (see p. 74, n. 31).

[34]MS *Grammont*.

[35]The name of this firm of merchants was Gramont Chegaray [& Cie], on the Pavé des Chartrons, nos. 11 & 12 (correspondence with the Chamber of Commerce, Bordeaux).

[36]So many plays dealing with this popular subject were produced from the fifteenth century to the nineteenth that it seems impossible to determine the particular one referred to here.

[37]Perhaps the romantic lyric drama *Paul et Virginie, ou Triomphe de la vertu* (words by Dubreuil, music by Lesueur), based on the well-known romance by Bernardin de Saint-Pierre, which was first produced in Paris in 1794.

[38]Jeanne Charlotte Schroeder (1764–1850), called Mme Saint-Aubin, well-known opera singer of the day.

23—Din[n]er with Mr. Perrot.[39]

24—Din[n]er at Camescasse['s] Country seat.[40] Supper with Riviere,[41] Morton,[42] Mr. Kean.[43]

25—Din[n]er at home. Mrs. Randall,[44] Mrs. Dabney.[45]

26—Din[n]er with Martini.[46] Saw Mr. Fleury Emery.[47]

---

[39]Probably a member of the Bordeaux firm of Perrot & Lee, which was engaged in the import and export business. William Lee (one of the partners), as successor to Isaac Cox Barnet, was to begin his service as U.S. consular agent, and later consul, at Bordeaux in Dec. 1801 (M. L. Mann, ed., *A Yankee Jeffersonian, Selections from the Diary and Letters of William Lee of Massachusetts, Written from 1796 to 1840* [Cambridge, Mass., 1958], p. 53). In 1804–1805 there were two Bordeaux firms (both with the same address) containing the name of Perrot, viz., Perrot & Binaud and Perrot & Lée [sic] (Duverneuil and La Tynna, *Almanach du commerce,* An XIII, p. 467).

[40]See p. 95, n. 31.

[41]Not identified, but it may be noted that in 1812 a firm named Rivière, ainé & Duboscq was listed among Bordeaux "Marchands en gros de rouenneries" (La Tynna, *Almanach du commerce,* Année 1812, p. 650).

[42]John A. Morton, of Baltimore, who appears among more than thirty "American merchants and shipmasters now at Bordeaux" who signed a testimonial, 20 July 1801, on behalf of Isaac Cox Barnet (Papers of Isaac Cox Barnet, Consular Despatches, Bordeaux, vol. I, Records of the Dept. of State, National Archives).

[43]MS Possibly *McKean.* Not identified.

[44]Not identified.

[45]Presumably the wife of John B. Dabney, of Boston, "a Citizen of the U.S. residing in Bordeaux" who is mentioned on p. 92, n. 12. He also appears among the "American merchants and shipmasters now in Bordeaux" who signed the testimonial, 20 July 1801, mentioned above. Later, on 27 June, Mrs. Dabney is described as "the fair American."

[46]The firm of Strobel & Martini appears in a long list of signatories (described as "Négociants établis à Bordeaux") of a testimonial on behalf of Isaac Cox Barnet, dated 27 Floréal An IX [17 May 1801] (Consular Despatches, Bordeaux, vol. I, Records of the Dept. of State, National Archives).

[47]He appears in the list of "Négociants établis à Bordeaux" cited in n. 46. He also appears in a list of Bordeaux "Armateurs et Négocian[t]s" for the year 1812 (La Tynna, *Almanach du commerce.* Année 1812, p. 648).

27—Din[n]er at home. Tea at Mrs. Tupper['s].[48] Mrs. Dabney, the fair American.[49]

28—Din[n]er at home. Supper at Mr. Muller['s].[50] Taken leave. I am to travel in a post chaise with McKim[51] and McElheny.[52]

29—Left Bordeaux at 10 A.M. Embarked on the river. Din[n]er at Blaye. Slept at Mirambeau.

30—Din[n]er at Saintes. Roman antiquities. Supper at Rochefort.

---

[48]Not identified.   [49]See p. 96, n. 45.   [50]See p. 95, n. 30.

[51]This may be Isaac McKim, of Baltimore, son of John McKim. It has not been possible to prove that he was in Bordeaux in 1801, but he was in close business relations with both Victor and E. I. du Pont from 1802 to 1805, and they used his services in the importation of powder-making machinery and other merchandise via the port of Baltimore (*Life of E. I. du Pont*, VI, 88, 90, 102, 103, 127, 162, 163, 237; VII, 163).

[52]Not identified. The Company Expense Account records that he and McKim were Victor's traveling companions all the way to Paris: "Journey from Bordeaux to Paris by Rochefort, Rochelle, Nantes, Angers, Saumur, Tours in a Post Charriot with McKim and McElheny—my third of the Post and tavern expenses amounted to..........682–12."

JULY

1—Din[n]er at Rochefort. Shell Inn. Seen Messrs. St. Clement,[1] Pelletreau.[2] Sup[p]er in [La] Rochelle.

2—Mr. Borde,[3] de Missy,[4] de Richemont,[5] Fair.

---

[1]François Pierre André Hèbre de Saint Clément (1759–1805), shipowner (armateur) and mayor of Rochefort (J. T. Viaud and E. J. Fleury, *Histoire de la ville et du port de Rochefort* [Rochefort, 1845], II, 440, 527).

[2]François Pelletreau (1760–1828), shipowner and merchant, living at 56 rue de la République, Rochefort (correspondence with the president of the Chamber of Commerce of Rochefort). The firm of François Pelletreau & Cie was listed among the merchants and shipowners at Rochefort in 1804–1805 (Duverneuil and La Tynna, *Almanach du commerce*, An XIII, p. 592).

[3]P. Borde, a shipping agent at La Rochelle from whom Victor, a few

3—Tivoli[6] at Mr. Trouard['s][7] gardens. Menoire[8] from Rochefort. Seen the English goods.

4—Left [La] Rochelle at 4 o'clock P.M. Slept at Maran[s] —6 leagues.

5—Slept at Nantes—29 leagues. Hotel de France, ci-dev[an]t Henry IV.

6—Seen Messrs. Rossel & Boudet.[9] Play house. Hamon,[10] Debree.[11]

---

weeks later, made inquiry concerning the shipping of salt from Ile de Ré to Bordeaux.

[4]Not identified, but it may be noted that a Demissy was listed among the "Négocian[t]s, armateurs, commissionnaires" of La Rochelle in 1804–1805 (Duverneuil and La Tynna, *Almanach du commerce*, An XIII, p. 594).

[5]In a letter to his father dated 22 May 1799 from La Rochelle, where he was seeking to promote the interest of Du Pont de Nemours, Père et Fils & Cie and obtain new shareholders, Victor speaks of the courtesies *(honnêtetés)* which he has received from his father's friends, Mr. de Richemont and Mr. de Trouard. Later in the same letter he says, "Mr. de Richemont a comme lui [Trouard] formé une manufacture de tabac dans un couvent de Carmes et comme lui l'a suspendue depuis l'impôt" (V. du P. to his father, 3 Prairial, An VII, Winterthur MSS).

[6]MS *Tivoly*. A game resembling bagatelle.

[7]A friend of du Pont de Nemours. (See a letter from Trouard to him, 25 March [1799], Winterthur MSS). In the letter from Victor to his father cited in n. 5, he speaks of the courtesies he has received from Trouard. Later in the same letter he says: "Mr. Trouard a formé dans un ci-devant couvent de Capucins un établissement superbe composé de deux manufactures, l'une de tabac, l'autre de vinaigres, eaux de vie, esprit de vins, et tout ce qui y a rapport." He adds details about the close relations which Trouard had with commercial interests on the Ile de Ré. His full name, however, and further details concerning him have not come to light.

[8]Alexis Guillaume Ménoire, brother of Mrs. Joseph Fenwick (see p. 52, n. 55, and pp. 64–65 and n. 65, 67). He had been assigned to Rochefort 31 May 1801 (correspondence with the Service Historique, French Ministry of War).

[9]The shipping firm of Rossel, Boudet & Cie of Nantes. Victor had repeated business dealings with them during his sojourn in France,

7—Left Nantes at 10 o'clock. Slept at Champtocé[12]—15 leagues. Broke the axle tree of our carriage.

8—Din[n]er at Angers. Slept at Saumur—17 leagues.

9—Slept at Blois—32 leagues.

10—Breakfast at Orleans. Arriv'd at Paris at 12 o'clock P.M.—45 leagues.

11—Din[n]er at Beauvilliers.[13] Mr. Roman.[14]

12—Din[n]er at Beauvilliers. Opera buffa.

13—Din[n]er at Beauvilliers. Mr. Hauterive.[15]

14—Din[n]er [with] Mrs. Fenwick.[16] Evening at the fête.[17]

15—Din[n]er with Melville.[18] Sup[p]er at Mrs. Tilden['s].[19]

16—Din[n]er at Mr. Duquesnoy['s].[20] Sup[p]er at Mrs. Killmaine['s].[21]

---

as numerous letters in the Eleutherian Mills Historical Library reveal (V. du P., Letter Book—1801, Winterthur MSS and Longwood MSS).

[10]William Hamon of Wilmington, one of Victor's fellow passengers on the voyage from New York to Le Havre. See p. 7, n. 19.

[11]Not identified, but it may be noted that a Brée was listed among the "Manufacturiers principaux" of Nantes in 1804–1805 (Duverneuil and La Tynna, *Almanach du commerce,* An XIII, p. 561).

[12]MS *Chantocé.* Champtocé-sur-Loire. On the page opposite this entry the author has made the following addition: "St. Georges Castle —of M. de Serent [*sic*], his son a dwarf." This Monsieur de Serrant was a descendant of Guillaume Bautru, Comte de Serrant (d. 1665), who acquired the Château de Serrant, near Saint-Georges-sur-Loire, in 1636. Dwarfism seems to have run in the family: the count's nephew had a son who was "une sorte de nain," and another nephew's daughter was "une vilaine fée, bossue, fort laide." See *Dictionnaire de biographie française,* under "Bautru."

[13]See p. 50, n. 39.   [14]See p. 24, n. 48.   [15]See p. 47, n. 21.

[16]See p. 52, n. 55 and pp. 64–65 and n. 65, 67.

[17]On the page opposite this entry the author has made the following addition: "14th, Parad[e] at the Castle [Château des Tuileries (?)], most magnificent display of troops, fête at the Champs Elysées."

[18]See p. 51, n. 47.   [19]See p. 36, n. 110.   [20]See p. 49, n. 33.

[21]Not identified. It would be pure conjecture to identify her as the widow of Charles Jennings Kilmaine (1751–1799), the distinguished

17—Din[n]er at Mrs. Lavoisier['s].

18—Din[n]er at Mr. Murray['s], our Minister plenipotentiary.[22]

19—Journey to Versailles. Water works.[23] Immense affluence of people; could not get in before 4 o['clock] in the morning.

20—Din[n]er at Beauvilliers with McKim.[24]

21—Din[n]er at Beauvilliers.

22—Din[n]er at Beauvilliers. Seen Duquesnoy.

23—Din[n]er at St. Cloud with Mrs. F[enwick]. Taken a Cabriolet by the month.

24—Din[n]er at Mrs.[25] de Caseaux['s].[26] Seen Mr. Hom.[27]

25—Din[n]er a[t] La Rapee.[28]

26—Din[n]er at Mr. de Lessert['s].[29] 7 Thermidor.[30]

French general of Irish origin who had also served in the War of American Independence.

[22]William Vans Murray (1760–1803), who had been a key figure in the negotiation of the convention of 1800, which ended the "Quasi War" between France and the U.S.

[23]Presumably a reference to the famous waterworks ("Machine de Marly"), located on the left bank of the Seine some five miles north of Versailles, which raised water from the river to an aqueduct which supplied the gardens and fountains of Versailles.

[24]His traveling companion in the post chaise from Bordeaux (see p. 97, n. 51).

[25]MS hardly legible; reading should possibly be *Mr.*

[26]Regarding her husband see p. 54, n. 67.

[27]Gilbert Hom, a small investor in the du Pont enterprises, who appears repeatedly in documents in the Eleutherian Mills Historical Library, usually without a first name. There are, however, several letters from Victor du Pont to him, 31 Aug., 16 Sept., and 18 Sept. 1801, in which he appears as G. or G[il]bert Hom (V. du P., Letter Book—1801, p. 54, Longwood MSS, and pp. 64–65, Winterthur MSS; *Life of E. I. du Pont, passim*).

[28]See p. 60, n. 34.

[29]See p. 31, n. 82.

[30]The date, 26 July 1801, was 7 Thermidor, but it is not clear why the author has inserted the phrase here. At the end of the line he has added three or four letters which may be *calv* but which seem to convey no meaning.

27—Din[n]er with Duquesnoy.[31] Seen Mr. de Fermont.[32]

28—Din[n]er with Reveroni.[33] Tea at Mrs. Murray['s].

29—Din[n]er with Mrs. Fenwick. Seen Mr. Necker Germany.[34]

30—Din[n]er at Beauvilliers.

31—Din[n]er at Beauvilliers.

---

[31]See p. 49 and n. 33.

[32]This may be Jacques Defermon des Chapelières (1752–1831), who had been a member of the National Constituent Assembly, the Convention, and the Council of Five Hundred. A warm supporter of Bonaparte, he was at the time of Victor's visit to Paris a member of the Council of State with special responsibilities in the financial department. He extended a warm welcome to du Pont de Nemours upon his arrival in Paris in 1802 (Kuscinski, *Dictionnaire des conventionnels;* B. G. du Pont, *Du Pont de Nemours,* II, 70).

[33]MS *Reverony* (see p. 30, n. 78).

[34]Louis Necker (1730–1804), called Necker de Germany or Necker Germany, elder brother of the more famous Jacques Necker, Minister of Finance under Louis XVI. Beginning life as a mathematician, he later entered the world of finance and became a millionaire through speculation. High hopes were entertained that he would be a large investor in the du Pont enterprises, but in the end his commitment seems to have been confined to a single share. The author was repeatedly in correspondence with him during his sojourn in France (J. C. Herold, *Mistress of an Age; A Life of Madame de Staël* [New York, 1958], pp. 4–5; *Life of E. I. du Pont, passim*).

AUGUST

1—Din[n]er at Beauvilliers with D'Autremont.[1]

2—Din[n]er at the Italians,[2] Nicole, with the Beliard[s].[3]

---

[1]See p. 66, n. 75.

[2]See p. 40, n. 125. It would seem that by sheer inadvertence the author made a very confusing entry here. What he probably intended to write was "Dinner at Nicole['s] with the Beliards. The Italians." In Day Book, Expences, the entry for this date is "Din[n]er with Beliards, 27 [livres]." Nicole was one of the well-known restaurants of the time, located at 11 boulevard des Italiens and therefore close to the Théâtre des Italiens.

[a]The author's reference to the Beliards here and elsewhere (pp. 64, 107, 113) is extremely confusing, since there is reason to believe that they are to be identified with the Vaubicourts, or Beliard Vaubicourts, to whom he makes reference elsewhere (pp. 110, 111, 113). It is also to be noted that following his return from France to America he received two letters written in an identical hand, 17 Jan., 15 March 1802. The first of these is signed "B V" and is endorsed in Victor du Pont's hand, "Vaubicour[t] Paris, Janvier 1802"; the second is signed "V" and is similarly endorsed, "Beliard Vaubicourt" (Beliard Vaubicourt to V. du P., 27 Nivôse An x and 24 Ventôse An x, Winterthur MSS). Also in Victor's account book marked "Ledger" there is record of a loan of 818 livres "on security doubtful" to "Beliard Vaubicour[t]."

A letter (30 Jan. 1961) received from the present General Louis de Vaubicourt, of Paris, gives quite specific information, evidently based on private family records, about the Belliard de Vaubicourt family in Victor du Pont's time. There were two brothers and a sister, children of Pierre Belliard de Vaubicourt of Paris (1728–1773), viz., Louis François (1766–1821); Pierre Jacques Nicolas (b. *ca.* 1770), who had a son named Victor; and Marie Antoinette Amélie (b. 10 Jan. 1770), who married a Mr. d'Ohsson, described as "ambassadeur de Suède," and who had no issue.

Assuming that these Belliard de Vaubicourts were the friends of the du Ponts whom the author refers to so confusingly, it may be conjectured that the younger of the two brothers was the one whom he saw repeatedly while in Paris, to whom he loaned money, and who wrote to him after his departure for America. In this connection it may be noted that this friend is described as without a profession ("pas de carrière") and that his son was named Victor. In the Day Book, Expences, the entry for 9 Aug. reads, "Christening Beliard child...106 [livres]." Was the child named for Victor du Pont?

The identification here proposed finds further support in records of the sister mentioned above. In an autograph summary of the principal events of his life to the year 1800, Victor du Pont records his "amours avec Amélie Beliard" just before his first journey to the United States in 1787, and upon his return at the end of 1790 he notes that he found her married (Winterthur MSS). Further, in the *Pocket Remembrancer*, 9 Oct., he makes the following entry: "Dinner at Vaubicourt['s]. Seen Mde d'O...since 10 years," and he records during the next four weeks five additional meetings with her (finally spelling her name d'Ohsson, in full). Victor du Pont does not mention her husband, but it can hardly be doubted that he was Ignace Mouradgea

French Bull fight.[4]

3—Din[n]er with the American Club.[5] Free Masons.[6]

4—Din[n]er with McKim[7] at Beauvilliers. Vaudeville.

5—Din[n]er at La Rapee.[8] Garden of Plants.[9] Tilden,[10]
Mr. Colignon,[11] etc.

6—Din[n]er with Mazuel.[12] Opera.

7—Din[n]er at Beauvilliers.

8—Din[n]er at Mr. de Lessert['s].[13] Seen Mr. Dolomieu,[14]

---

d'Ohsson (1740–1807), well-known historian of the Ottoman Empire.
Though of Armenian ancestry, he became a Swedish citizen, was
decorated with the Order of Vasa (1782), and served as Swedish
minister in Constantinople from 1795 to 1799. It was in 1787 that he
assumed the name d'Ohsson, deriving it from an uncle in his father's
family.

[4]In this period bullfights, not uncommon in the south of France,
were occasionally tolerated in Paris. Public controversy concerning
them appears in the Paris press.

[5]See p. 45.

[6]The author was a Freemason. He mentions the order again on 21
and 27 Oct. Further information about his contact with them may be
gained from the following entries in his Day Book, Expences: "August 3, Masons 78"; "September 12, alms at Lodge 3, Macon(?) scroll(?)
5"; "September 16, alms Macons 1–10"; "October 27, Alms to lodge 3";
"November 1st, Lodge acc't & certificate 75." Finally in Victor's Classified Expense Account there is a list headed "1801 Various Expences
in France, needful, incidental & unavoidable" in which we read
"Masons lodge Reception & alms...180." There is some inconsistency in the foregoing figures; but of Victor's active connection with
the Freemasons in Paris from July 1801 until his departure in early
Nov. there can be no doubt. He remained an active Mason upon his
return to America and in June 1825 was elected Grand Treasurer of
the Grand Lodge of Delaware.

[7]See p. 97, n. 51.   [8]See p. 60, n. 34.

[9]The Jardin des Plantes was almost opposite the quai de la Rapée
on the other side of the river.

[10]See p. 35, n. 109.   [11]Not identified.

[12]Not identified.   [13]See p. 31, n. 82.

[14]Presumably Déodat Guy Sylvain Tancrède Gratet de Dolomieu
(1750–1801), celebrated geologist and mineralogist and fellow member,
with du Pont de Nemours, of the Institute. At the end of an undated

Necker Germany.[15] Seen show at Louvois,[16] Picard['s][17] new play.

9—Din[n]er at Beauvilliers. Tivoli.[18]

10—Din[n]er at Beauvilliers.

11—Din[n]er at Mr. De L'Orme['s].[19]

12—Din[n]er at Beauvilliers. Mr. Murray[20] gone.

13—Din[n]er at Beauvilliers. Tisane.[21] Mr. [de] Ternant[22] arrives.

14—Din[n]er at Beauvilliers with Mr. de Ternant.

15—Din[n]er at Beauvilliers.

16—Din[n]er at Mr. Lamotte['s].[23]

17—Din[n]er at Very['s].[24] Tuileries.

18—Din[n]er at Beauvilliers.

---

letter by Latour-Maubourg (another member of the Institute) to du Pont de Nemours in New York, the sentence is added: "Dolomieu vient de mourir" (Winterthur MSS). Dolomieu had gone as a scientist on Bonaparte's expedition to Egypt in 1798, had been captured and imprisoned at Messina, Sicily, on his way home, had been released in March 1801, and had returned to France where he died 26 Nov. 1801.

[15]See p. 101, n. 34.

[16]The Théâtre Louvois, 8 rue Louvois.

[17]Louis Benoît Picard (1769–1828), playwright, actor, and producer who about the year 1800 assumed the direction of the Théâtre Louvois and achieved there, with his wife and brother, an outstanding success. The play in question was *Duhautcours, ou Le contrat d'union.*

[18]MS *Tivoly.* The reference is presumably to the celebrated amusement park in the quartier de l'Europe.

[19]Marion De L'Orme (see p. 39, n. 124).

[20]See p. 100, n. 22.

[21]MS *Tisan.* There are not infrequent references in the author's account books to the purchase of this infusion.

[22]Jean de Ternant (1740–1816), French minister to the U.S., 1791–1793, with whom Victor had sailed to America as second secretary of legation in 1791 *(Correspondence of the French Ministers to the United States, 1791–1797,* ed. F. J. Turner, in American Historical Association, *Annual Report for the Year 1903* [Washington, 1904], II, 43, n. *b; Life of E. I. du Pont,* I, 147, 148).

[23]A cousin of the author (see p. 41, n. 132).

[24]A celebrated restaurant of the epoch located in the Jardin des Tuileries.

19—Din[n]er at Beauvilliers.

20—Din[n]er at Mr. Tilden['s].[25]

21—Din[n]er at Beauvilliers.

22—Din[n]er at Beauvilliers.

23—Din[n]er at Brevannes.[26] Mr. Brousse, Mde Reverony.[27] Bal.

24—Din[n]er at Sauvo['s].[28]

25—Din[n]er at Beauvilliers.

26—Din[n]er at Beauvilliers. G[ener]al Clarke.[29]

27—Din[n]er at Beauvilliers. Consul Le Brun.

28—Din[n]er at Mr. de Lessert['s].

29—Din[n]er at Beauvilliers.

30—Din[n]er at Beauvilliers with Grant[30] and Waddel.[31]

31—Din[n]er at Mr. Adet['s].[32]

---

[25]See p. 35, n. 109.

[26]A village in the department of Seine-et-Oise a short distance south of Paris.

[27]It may perhaps be conjectured that *Mde Reverony* is an error for *Mde de Rumilly.*

[28]François Sauvo (1772–1859), who in 1800 was made editor of the *Moniteur* and who is credited with having done much to improve the quality and broaden the interest of this famous official newspaper. His wife, Marie Bonne Houdar de Lamotte, was a distant cousin of E. I. du Pont (*Life of E. I. du Pont,* VIII, 176–181, where Sauvo's initial is given erroneously as *N*).

[29]Presumably Henry Jacques Guillaume Clarke (1765–1818), who became Comte d'Hunebourg in 1808, Duc de Feltre in 1809, and a peer of France in 1814.

[30]See p. 38, n. 120.

[31]See p. 38, n. 119.

[32]Pierre Auguste Adet (1763–1832), who was appointed minister to the U.S. in 1795 and took Victor with him as first secretary of legation (*Correspondence of the French Ministers to the United States, 1791–1797,* II, 728, n. *b*).

SEPTEMBER

1—Din[n]er at Mr. Tochon['s],[1] Boulogne.[2] Mr. Homberg.[3]

2—Din[n]er at Mr. La Fore[s]t['s].[4]

3—Din[n]er at Mrs. Rangnon['s].[5] Mde la Crosse[6] and [Mde?][7] Grandmaison.

4—Din[n]er at Beauvilliers.

5—Din[n]er at Beauvilliers. Mr. Mandeville,[8] sec[retar]y of Mr. Mer[r]y.[9]

---

[1] Joseph François Tochon (see p. 50 and n. 36, and p. 53).

[2] Boulogne-sur-Seine, to the west of Paris, where Tochon's country seat was located.

[3] Probably Grégoire Homberg, Tochon's father-in-law (see p. 17, n. 22, and p. 50, n. 36).

[4] MS *La Foret.* Possibly Antoine René Charles Mathurin, Comte de La Forest (1756–1846), the well-known French diplomat who had been in America several times and was, under Talleyrand's patronage, entrusted with heavy responsibilities during the early years of the Consulate.

[5] Not identified.

[6] Possibly the wife of Admiral Jean Raymond, Baron de Lacrosse (1760–1829), who in 1801 had been sent as colonial prefect and captain general to Guadeloupe.

[7] Presumably Mme Grandmaison, since she appears twice more a few lines farther on. Efforts to identify her have been unsuccessful. Joseph Marie Jouve de Grandmaison (1762–1839), a fairly active member of the Council of Five Hundred in the period of the Directory, may have been her husband.

[8] Not otherwise identified.

[9] Anthony Merry, who is described in the entry for 16 Sept. as "the British envoy." He had spent twenty-three years in Spain, part of the time as consul general and as chargé d'affaires. He was soon to be secretary of legation to Lord Cornwallis in the negotiation of the Treaty of Amiens (1802) and British minister to the U.S., 1803–1806 (Elizabeth Donnan and L. F. Stock, eds., *An Historian's World. Selections from the Correspondence of John Franklin Jameson* [Philadelphia, 1956], p. 261, n. 338, 340). The *Moniteur*, 9 July 1801, announced his arrival in Paris as the "nouveau commissaire anglais pour l'échange des prisonniers de cette nation." The preliminaries of peace between Britain and France were not signed in London until 1 Oct.

6—Gone to St. Leu[10] at Mr. Homberg['s] with Mr. Beliard[11] and Brousse.[12] Beautifull seat. Gardens etc.

7—Din[n]er at Mr. Bernardin de St. Pierre['s].[13]

8—Din[n]er at Harmand['s].[14] Mde Grandmaison.

9—Din[n]er at Swan['s],[15] Passy. Mr. Dumas of Hamburg.[16]

10—Din[n]er at Mde Grandmaison['s]. Mr. —— [name omitted by author].

11—Din[n]er at Leda['s][17] with Mrs. T[ilden].[18]

12—Din[n]er at Beauvilliers.

13—Din[n]er at St. Cloud. Great fête.[19]

14—Din[n]er at La Rapee[20] with T[ilden?].

15—Din[n]er at Beauvilliers. Gone to[21] Malmaison.[22] Seen Mde Bonaparte.

16—Din[n]er at Mandeville['s],[23] secretary of the British envoy.[24]

17—Din[n]er at Beauvilliers. Gone to[25] Boulogne. Mr. Forfait,[26] Minister of Marine.[27]

---

[10]Probably St.-Leu-la-Forêt, department of Seine-et-Oise, a few miles northwest of Paris. It may be conjectured that one of the Hombergs had a country seat there.

[11]See p. 102, n. 3.   [12]See p. 32, n. 88.

[13]Presumably Jacques Henri Bernardin de St. Pierre (1737–1814), the famous French naturalist and author, who in 1800 married, as his second wife, Marguerite Charlotte Désirée de la Fite de Pelleport (1780–1847), a niece of Mme Victor du Pont.

[14]See p. 23, n. 46.   [15]See p. 58, n. 24.   [16]Not identified.

[17]See p. 52, n. 56.   [18]See p. 36, n. 110.

[19]The famous annual fair at St.-Cloud, for an extraordinary description of which see Larousse, *Grand dictionnaire universel du XIX siècle*, under "Foire." In his Day Book, Expences, for 13 Sept. Victor records an outlay of 18 livres for dinner and four for "parc tickets."

[20]See p. 60, n. 34.   [21]MS *at*.

[22]The chateau at Rueil-Malmaison, western suburb of Paris. It was the residence of Bonaparte and Josephine from 1800 to 1803 and of the latter after her divorce in 1809.

[23]See p. 106, n. 8.   [24]See p. 106, n. 9.   [25]MS *at*.

[26]MS *Forfaix*. See p. 48, n. 25.

[27]In his Day Book, Expences, 20 Sept., Victor has made the following

18—Din[n]er at Waddel['s].[28]

19—Din[n]er at Beauvilliers.

20—Din[n]er at Rose's.[29] Vaudeville.

21—Din[n]er at Rose's.

22—Din[n]er at Mr. Hom['s].[30] Emery,[31] Hauterive.[32] Seen Mrs. Chastel.[33]

23—Din[n]er at the Thuileries. Great fete. 1st Vendemiaire.[34]

24—Din[n]er at home.

25—Gone in the stage to Nemours. Slept at Egreville[35] at Bernier['s].[36]

26—Bois des Fossés. Nursery of American trees.

---

puzzling entry: "Pigeons for the minister, 15 [livres]." It may be conjectured that this was a small gift for Forfait, Minister of Marine, whom he had visited at Boulogne-sur-Seine three days previously, and whose official influence he was seeking in favor of Du Pont de Nemours, Père et Fils & Cie. For evidence that he was cultivating Mrs. Tilden to this same end, see p. 36, n. 110.

[28]See p. 38, n. 119.

[29]One of the half-dozen best Paris restaurants of the time. The name is derived from a chef formerly in the service of the aristocracy (Biré, *Diary of a Citizen of Paris during the Terror*, II, 334).

[30]See p. 100, n. 27.

[31]Possibly, though by no means certainly, Fleury Emery. See p. 96, n. 47.

[32]See p. 47, n. 21.

[33]Not identified.

[34]La Fête de la Fondation de la République, celebrated at the beginning of the French Revolutionary calendar year. In 1801 an important feature was a water spectacle held on the Seine between the Pont des Tuileries (Pont Royal) and the Pont de la Concorde, which explains the author's choice of a dining place at the Tuileries. See the description of the fête in the *Moniteur*, 3 Vendémiaire An x.

[35]Égreville, a short distance beyond Nemours on the way to Bois-des-Fossés.

[36]Bernier, a lawyer of Égreville, was an intimate friend and neighbor of the du Pont family. Victor du Pont was present at his wedding. In spite of the numerous references to him in du Pont correspondence, his first name remains undetermined (*Life of E. I. du Pont, passim*).

27—Din[n]er at Branles[37] at Mrs. Dufay['s].[38] Returned to[39] Nemours.

28—Arrived in Paris at 5 o'clock. Dined at home.

29—Din[n]er at Beauvilliers. Louvois, La petite ville.[40]

30—Din[n]er at Beauvilliers. Visits.

[37]A small village near Égreville.

[38]The Dufays of Branles were close neighbors and friends of the du Ponts (Life of E. I. du Pont, passim). Their first names have not been determined.

[39]MS at.

[40]In 1801 the celebrated playwright, Louis Benoît Picard (1769–1828), produced at the Théâtre Louvois (see p. 104, n. 16) La petite ville, in prose, which is described as one of his chefs-d'oeuvre.

OCTOBER

1—Din[n]er at Mde de Chastel['s].[1] Great talk of peace.[2] Stock jobbing.

2—Din[n]er at Mr. de Marbois['s].[3] Petit de Villers[4] arrived.

3—Din[n]er at Beauvilliers.

4—Din[n]er at Beauvilliers. Peace proclaimed very unexpected[ly][5] and received very indiferently.

5—Din[n]er at Mr. La Forest['s][6] with Mess[rs.] Pinckney,[7]

[1]Not identified.

[2]Peace between France and Britain. The Preliminaries of London were signed in London on 1 Oct., and the Peace of Amiens was finally concluded in March 1802.

[3]François Barbé-Marbois (1745–1837). See p. 24, n. 49.

[4]See p. 11 and n. 38.

[5]The Preliminaries of London.

[6]See p. 106, n. 4.

[7]Probably Charles Pinckney (1757–1824), the newly appointed U.S. minister to Spain who made a leisurely journey through the Netherlands and France en route to Madrid, where he arrived 8 Dec. 1801. This was likely the Pinckney with whom Victor du Pont dined in Bordeaux on 12 Nov. (see p. 114), since we know from a letter of David Humphreys, written from Madrid, 6 Nov. 1801, that Charles Pinckney was expected to be soon in Bordeaux on his way to Spain

Barthelemy,[8] S[ie]yes,[9] Marbois.

6—Din[n]er at Beauvilliers.

7—Din[n]er at Mr. Dallarde['s].[10]

8—Din[n]er at Tochon['s],[11] Boulogne.

9—Din[n]er at Vaubicourt['s].[12] Seen Mde d'O[hsson]...
since 10 years.[13]

10—Din[n]er at Bro[n]gn[i]art['s].[14] Manufactury of
Sev[r]es.

11—Din[n]er at Mr. [De] Lessert['s][15] with Mr. Pinckney,
Gore,[16] Brillat S[avarin?].[17]

(Humphreys, *Life and Times of David Humphreys,* II, 335–337). It is
not improbable (though it is, of course, not certain) that he might
have been at La Forest's dinner in Paris on 5 Oct. It is, however,
possible that the dinner guest was not Charles Pinckney but William
Pinkney (1764–1822), of Maryland, one of the joint commissioners
who had been appointed by Washington under the terms of the Jay
Treaty to negotiate the settlement of American claims for maritime
losses. He remained in London for some eight years, and it may be
presumed that the preliminaries of peace between France and Britain
(1 Oct. 1801) would have opened the way for his presence in France
at this time.

[8]Presumably François, Marquis de Barthélemy (1750–1830), French
diplomat and politician, who had been elected a member of the
Executive Directory in 1796. He had been expelled by the coup d'état
of 18 Fructidor 1797, imprisoned, and exiled to French Guiana. From
there he escaped to the U.S. and then to England. With the rise of
Bonaparte to power he returned to France and to high favor.

[9]Probably Emmanuel Joseph Sieyès (1748–1836), French abbé,
cautious politician, and constitutional theorist who had repeatedly
played a prominent role in the Revolution and, though a member of
the Executive Directory in its last year, had played a leading part
in its overthrow. Like Barthélemy he was a member of the Senate
under the Consulate.

[10]Pierre Gilbert Leroi, Baron d'Allarde (1749–1809). See p. 60, n. 33.

[11]Joseph François Tochon, whose country place was at Boulogne-
sur-Seine (see p. 50 and n. 36, and pp. 53, 60).

[12]See p. 102, n. 3.   [13]See p. 102, n. 3.

[14]Alexandre Brongniart. See p. 45, n. 12.

[15]See p. 31, n. 82.

12—Din[n]er at Mr. Homberg['s], St. Leu Taverny.[18]

13—Din[n]er at Mr. Terson['s].[19] Even[in]g, Vaubi[court] with Mde d'O[hsson].[20]

14—Din[n]er at Mr. Bro[n]gn[i]art['s]. Fourcroy,[21] G[ener]al Boudet.[22]

15—Breakfast at 9 [o']clock with Regnault de St. Jean d'Angely.[23] Gone to Versailles. Mde d'Ohsson. Slept there.

16—Din[n]er at Consul Le Brun's. 7 heures (?) $\frac{1}{2}$.[24] G[ener]al Kellermann,[25] Benezech,[26] Council[or] of State.

17—Din[n]er at Mr. de Marbois['s].

---

[16]Possibly Christopher Gore (1758–1827), of Massachusetts, who in 1796, with William Pinkney, was appointed commissioner to England under the Jay Treaty to settle American claims for maritime losses (see p. 109, n. 7).

[17]Conceivably Anthelme Brillat-Savarin (1755–1826), lawyer, economist, and gastronomist, who was to become famous through his witty treatise on the art of dining, *La physiologie du goût* (Paris, 1825). At the time of Victor's journey he was a member of the Court of Cassation. At the beginning of the Revolution he had been a member, like du Pont de Nemours, of the National Constituent Assembly. No other evidence has come to light indicating a contact between him and any of the du Ponts.

[18]Presumably St.-Leu-la-Forêt, close by Taverny, department of Seine-et-Oise, where one of the Hombergs had his country home.

[19]Not identified.

[20]See p. 102, n. 3.

[21]Possibly Antoine François, Comte de Fourcroy (1755–1809), whose *Rapport...au nom du Comité de Salut Public sur les arts...et sur le nouveau procédé de tannage découvert par le citoyen Armand Séguin* was published by the Du Pont Press in the year III (1794–1795). In 1803 E. I. du Pont in America wrote his father in Paris that he could not find a copy of this work, which he wanted *(Life of E. I. du Pont,* VI, 212).

[22]Jean, Comte Boudet (1769–1809), one of the distinguished generals of the revolutionary and Napoleonic epoch (Six, *Dictionnaire biographique des généraux & amiraux français).*

[23]See p. 44, n. 7.

[24]Presumably the author has fallen into French for the dinner hour 7:30, but the manuscript reading of *heures* is uncertain.

[25]Probably François Christophe de Kellermann (1735–1820), hero

18—Din[n]er at Brevannes.[27] Brousse.

19—Din[n]er at home with Mrs. T[ilden].[28]

20—Din[n]er at Beauvilliers. Mrs. d'Ohss[on].

21—Din[n]er at Beauvilliers with Digneron[29] and Petit [de Villers]. Macons.[30]

22—Din[n]er at Mr. de Lessert['s] with Mess[rs] Van Staphorst, etc.[31] Vaubi[court], d'Ohsson.[32]

23—Din[n]er at Mr. de L'Orme['s].[33] Theatre Feydeau.[34]

24—Din[n]er at Beauvilliers.

25—Din[n]er at Beauvilliers.

---

of the battle of Valmy, who in 1800 was made a senator by Bonaparte, a marshal of France in 1803, and Duke of Valmy in 1808. His son, François Étienne de Kellermann (1770–1835), the famous Napoleonic cavalry officer, was also a general at this time, but it seems less likely that he would have been in Paris.

[26]Pierre Bénézech (1749–1802), a conservative politician and administrator who had risen to the position of Minister of the Interior in 1795 under the Directory, had been dismissed but escaped deportation in 1797, and had been made a Councilor of State by Bonaparte at the end of 1799. He was sent as a colonial prefect to Santo Domingo in 1802 and died there of yellow fever.

[27]See p. 63, n. 26.   [28]See p. 36, n. 110.   [29]Not identified.

[30]Freemasons. See p. 103, n. 6.

[31]Evidently a member, or members, of the firm of Messrs. Van Staphorst & Co., of Amsterdam, to which firm Victor had written 23 July asking insurance on a shipment of laces, valued at "[£?]3020 17s 9[d?]," via the ship *L'olive*, to New York (V. du P., Letter Book—1801, p. 30, Winterthur MSS). This wealthy firm had been connected with American financial affairs since 1792, when it assisted in floating the first Dutch loan to the U.S. Apparently the members of the firm in 1801 were Nicolaas and Jacob Van Staphorst and possibly Nicolaas Hubbard (P. J. Van Winter, *Het Aandeel van den Amsterdamschen handel aan den opbouw van het Amerikaansche Gemeenebest* [The Hague, 1933], II, 333).

[32]MS *dhos.*

[33]MS *de Lorme.* See p. 39, n. 124.

[34]Also called Théâtre de l'Opéra-Comique, located at 19 rue Feydeau. The plays presented on this date were *Les événemens imprévus* and *Les visitandines.*

26—Din[n]er at Melville['s].[35] Consul Cambacerès.
27—Din[n]er with the Macons.[36] Reception.
28[37]—Din[n]er at Beauvilliers.
29—Din[n]er at General Kellermann['s].[38]
30—Din[n]er at Mr. Terson['s].[39]
31—[Dinner] at Beauvilliers with Petit [de Villers].

[35]See p. 51, n. 47.
[36]See p. 103, n. 6.
[37]In both the Day Book, Expences and the Company Expense Account for this date we note an entry which in its fuller form reads: "Mounting a little engraving of G[ener]al Washington for Mrs. Bonaparte, 15 [livres]". It will be remembered that Victor had called upon her at Malmaison on 15 Sept.
[38]See p. 111, n. 25.
[39]See p. 111, n. 19.

NOVEMBER

1—Din[n]er at Nicole['s].[1] Italians. Mr. Digneron.[2]
2—Din[n]er at Mr. Roman['s].[3] Petit [de Villers] and Villars gone.[4]
3—Din[n]er at Beauvilliers at 10 o'clock.
4—Din[n]er at Mr. Terson['s].
5—Din[n]er at Beauvilliers with Beliard and Vaubicourt, Mrs. d'Ohsson.[5]
6—Left Paris in the diligence at 10 o'clock A.M. Supper at Etampes. Gone all night.
7—Din[n]er at Orleans. Supper at Blois.
8—Din[n]er at Tours. Supper at Ste. Maure.[6] Gone all night.
9—Detestable roads. Left the diligence at Poitiers to take the mail [coach].

[1]See p. 101, n. 2.
[2]See p. 112, n. 29.
[3]See p. 24, n. 48.
[4]Presumably they had set out for Bordeaux to be ready for the sailing of the *Benjamin Franklin.*
[5]See p. 102, n. 3.
[6]Ste.-Maure-de-Touraine, department of Indre-et-Loire.

10—Supper at Angoulême.

11—Breakfast at Barbezieux.[7] Slept at Cubzac.[8]

12—Arrived at Bordeaux at 10 o'clock. Din[n]er at Mr. Th[eodore] Peters[']9 with Mr. Pinckney.[10] Lodge at the Franklin.

13—Din[n]er at Barnet['s].[11] Blandin.[12] La Chapelle.[13]

14—Din[n]er at Mr. de Gramont['s].[14]

15—[Dinner] at home with Dewe[e]s.[15] Comedy.

---

[7] MS *Barbesieux.*

[8] MS *Cussac.* It seems probable that this is a misspelling of Cubzac (St.-André-de-Cubzac, Gironde), on the road from Barbezieux to Bordeaux.

[9] Presumably Theodore Peters, who was described in 1796 as "one of the first merchants of Bordeaux." A native of Holland, he had fled to Bordeaux on account of his political principles. By industry and good fortune he had risen from poverty to wealth and the ownership of a country estate (Mann, ed., *A Yankee Jeffersonian,* pp. 11, 15–16).

[10] Charles Pinckney (1757–1824), then on his way to Madrid (see p. 109, n. 7).

[11] The author first wrote *Barney* and then corrected it by striking *tt* over the *y* to make *Barnett.* This was Isaac Cox Barnet, who had been consul at Brest until Dec. 1798, when he was made consular agent at Bordeaux (see the Isaac Cox Barnet papers, Records of the Dept. of State, Commissions: Consuls and Consular Agents, National Archives).   [12] See p. 73, n. 28.

[13] Not identified, but it may be noted that an imperial decree, 24 March 1808, names a M. LaChapelle "secrétaire en chef de la mairie de Bordeaux, aux fonctions de membre du conseil de préfecture du département de la Gironde" *(Moniteur,* 8 May 1808, p. 508).

[14] MS *Grammont.* Probably a member of the firm of Gramont & Cie, merchants of Bordeaux. The firm name appears underneath a testimonial on behalf of Isaac Cox Barnet, 21 Oct. 1801 (Consular Despatches, Bordeaux, vol. I, Records of the Dept. of State, National Archives). He may also have been a member of the Conseil Général of the department of the Gironde *(Almanach national,* An x, p. 300).

[15] Presumably Jesse Dewees, whose name appears among those of more than thirty "American merchants and shipmasters then at Bordeaux" beneath the testimonial on behalf of Isaac Cox Barnet, cited on p. 96, n. 42.

16—Saw the Prefe[c]t,[16] The American Consul,[17] Mr. Perrot.[18] Dined at home. Gone to the Cercle.[19]

17—Din[n]er at home. Play, Vestris[20] and Chameroy.[21] Ball at Cercle.

18—Din[n]er at a restaurateur with La Chapelle,[22] Loup,[23] La Neuville.[24]

19—Din[n]er with Mess[rs.] Blandin [Frères].[25] Play with Petit [de Villers].

20—Din[n]er at home alone.

21—Din[n]er at the 7 Brothers Masons,[26] with La Chapelle, Camescasse,[27] La Neuville, Loup.

22—Din[n]er at home with Dewe[e]s, Wilson,[28] Morton,[29] Nott,[30] Petit [de Villers].

---

[16]His name was Dubois (des Vosges), according to the *Almanach national*, An x.

[17]The American consular agent, Isaac Cox Barnet, with whom he had dined 13 Nov. (see p. 114, n. 11).

[18]See p. 96, n. 39.

[19]Probably the Cercle des Chartrons (see p. 94, n. 28).

[20]The celebrated dancer, Marie Auguste Vestris (1760–1842), sometimes called Vestris II and sometimes, in order to include the names of both his famous dancing parents, Vestris-Allard.

[21]Marie Adrienne Chameroy (1779–1802), the famous danseuse of the Paris Opéra.

[22]See p. 114, n. 13.

[23]Not identified.

[24]Not identified, though in a letter from Victor du Pont, Rochefort, to his brother Irénée, 11 June 1791, he says: "I will write to...Mr. La Neuville" *(Life of E. I. du Pont*, I, 146).

[25]See p. 73, n. 28.

[26]According to M. Xavier Védère, of Bordeaux, Departmental Archivist of the Gironde, there was, about 1801, a Hôtel des Sept Frères Maçons" at 5 rue de l'Intendance (now rue Guillaume Brochon), Bordeaux.

[27]See p. 95, n. 31.

[28]Not identified.

[29]John A. Morton, of Baltimore (see p. 96, n. 42).

[30]William Nott, of Charleston, who was among the "American merchants and shipmasters then in Bordeaux" who signed a testimonial

23—Din[n]er at Mr. Martini['s].[31] Little théâtre.[32]

24—Ship goes down the river.[33] Din[n]er at a restaurateur.

25—Din[n]er at home with General Faucher.[34]

26—Din[n]er at home with Dewe[e]s, Faucher,[35] Nott.

27—Din[n]er at Mr. Perrot's.[36]

28—Din[n]er at home.

29—Left Bordeaux in a boat at 11 o'clock A.M.[37] Bad weather, great difficulty to get on board.[38]

---

20 July 1801 on behalf of Isaac Cox Barnet (see the document cited above, p. 96, n. 42).

[31]Perhaps a member of the firm of Strobel & Martini (see p. 96, n. 46).

[32]MS *theathre*.

[33]The *Benjamin Franklin* on which Victor was about to sail. In his last letter to his wife before sailing, Bordeaux 15 Nov. and sent by the *Cérès*, Victor says: "Enfin ma chère, je suis ici, mes affaires finies, mes malles faites, prêt à m'embarquer sur le Franklin qui part, dit on, dans 5 ou 6 jours" (V. du P. to Mme V. du P., 15 Nov. [1801], Winterthur MSS). Bordeaux is some sixty miles up the river from the sea. It was necessary to take advantage of the tide to get downstream and then await favorable winds before sailing. Du Pont preferred to remain at Bordeaux until nearer sailing time.

[34]MS *Fauchet*. General Pierre Jean Marie (called Constantin) de Faucher (1760–1815), who at this time was sous-préfet of La Réole, Gironde (Six, *Dictionnaire biographique des généraux & amiraux français*). A letter from Faucher to du Pont de Nemours, 7 Frimaire x [28 Nov. 1801], makes it certain that Victor du Pont was in touch with him at this time (Winterthur MSS).

[35]MS *Fauchet*.

[36]See p. 96, n. 39.

[37]The following outlays made during Victor's last weeks in France in preparation for his journey home may be noted from the Day Book, Expences:

2 Mattrasses	60
1 Pillar	10
2 Blankets	16–4
Nitted waistcoat	12
Pair of gloves	4
Napkins for [a]board	21
A shirt for Villars	10

30—Went ashore to Pauillac.[39] Good din[n]er at Miss Cadette['s] tavern.

Trousers for Villars	8
Emballage pour ditto et droits	42–11
Pair of gloves	10
Shoes for myself	6
ditto for Villars	6
Provisions in Bordeaux	589–10
Passage	650
Sup[p]lement provisions in the River	30
25 Bottles Cognac brandy	77–15

[38]To board the *Franklin* which was anchored down river.
[39]MS *Pouilhac.*

DECEMBER

1—Staid ashore with great company of several vessels bound to Louisiana, Cayenne, Guadeloupe, Isle de France, etc. (?)[1]

2—Staid at Pauillac.[2] Mr. Poignant of New Orleans.[3]

3—D[itt]o d[itt]o. Rainy weather.

4—D[itt]o d[itt]o. Detestable country, half savages.

5—D[itt]o d[itt]o. The post goes to Bordeaux when it does not rain.

6—Slept on board. Got a cold in my head.

7—Went a-shooting.

8—Rainy weather. Tiedious time.

9—The same thing.

10—Determined to go back to Bordeaux with Peters,[4] Capt. Martin.[5]

11—Left Pauillac[6] at 3 o'clock A.M. No wind. Staid all day at Bec d'Ambès.[7] Several Captains and passengers.

12—Arrived at Bordeaux at 2 A.M. Hotel Franklin.

[1]The reading *etc.* is not certain.   [2]MS *Pouilhac.*
[3]Not identified, but perhaps a passenger on a vessel bound for Louisiana.
[4]See p. 114, n. 9.   [5]Not identified.   [6]MS *Pouilhac.*
[7]Bec d'Ambès is located below Bordeaux at the confluence of the Garonne and the Dordogne rivers.

Addendum [Dec. 1801

13—Bad weather. Din[n]er at home with G[ener]al Faucher,[8] Dewe[e]s, etc. Bal.

14—The wind changes, great deal of rain.

15—Went down to Pauillac.[9] The boatman run us ashore on a bank in the river. Arrived at night.

16—Slept at LaDette.[10] Our ship goes down early in the morning. Ran after her in a boat. Slept on board.

17—Went down the river. The pilot run the ship ashore on Marguerite Bank[11] where she staid 8 hours.

18—Went to sleep at Royan. Awaked in the night to go on board, fair wind, nearly loosing my passage.

19—Left the pilot 4 leagues south of Cordouan[12] at 12 o'clock. N.E. wind.

20—Came up with all the vessels which had sailed 3 hours before us. S.W. winds.

21—Calms.

22—Easterly winds, light breezes.

23—Cloudy weather. Westerly winds.

24—Squalls. Westerly winds, heavy seas.

25—Blow a gale of West. Very high seas. Lay to.

26—D[itt]o 30 hours.

27—W.S.W. winds. Rough seas. Saw a ship standing on same tack. Passed her.

28—Same bad winds. Very heavy sea. Going to the northward.

29—Same. Cloudy weather. Very rough sea. Squalls. Gone 10 knots.

30—W.N.W. winds. Gone southward. Same squally weather. Blow very hard.

31—N. East winds, fine weather, 9 k[no]ts.

---

[8]MS *Fauchet*.

[9]MS *Pouilhac*.

[10]The location of this place remains undetermined.

[11]The shoals known as Banc des Marguerites inside the river entrance from the sea.

[12]The rock and lighthouse of Cordouan, some 6 or 7 miles west of Royan.

Addendum

JANUARY

1—Latit[u]d[e]42° 15′. Fine weather. Smooth sea. Easterly winds.

2—Fine weather, fine breeze of N.E. All sails out. Steer S.W. by S.

3—Superb weather, fine breeze 9 and 10 knots. Abreast of St. Mary[1] in the night.

4—35° 47′ Lat[itude] ob[served]. Squally but fine winds. Stearing W. by S.

5—Same good weather and northwardly winds. Saw a sail.

6—Same fine warm weather. Came up with the ship we saw. Easterly winds.

7—Lat[itude] obs[erve]d 31° 27′. Ship close to us. Calms in the night. Westerly winds.

8—Squally weather, N.W. winds.

9—Lat[itude] ob[served] 30° 16′. Same winds.

10—Squally weather. Same winds.

11—Lat[itude] obs[erved] 26° 21′. Fine warm weather.

12—Wind north.

13—Easterly winds. Fine warm weather. Lat[itude] obs[erved] 24° 5′.

14—South winds.

15—Variable winds. Great swell from the northwest.

16—North winds. Same heavy sea from the northward.

17—Lat[itude] obs[erve]d 22° 30′. Saw a schooner standing south. 22 degrees of longit[ude] these 7[2] days past.

18—Lat[itude] 22°. Longitud[e] 56° 10′. North winds. Fine weather, but cold for the climate.

19—Christening the passengers.

20—North and variable winds.

21—Fine weather. N.N.E. winds. Lat[itude] obs[erved] 25°. Long[itude] 63° 54′.

[1]The island of Santa Maria in the southeastern part of the Azores.

[2]The author first wrote *8* and then wrote *7* over it. What he appears to mean is that they had sailed over a distance of 22 degrees of longitude within the past week.

22—E[a]st winds. Spoke sloop Delight of Baltimore 10 days out: moderate winter in America.

23—Very light Breezes from the S.E. Saw a schooner.

24—Calms. Hazy weather.

25—North winds and calms. Squalls and calms.

26—Fine weather. North light winds, calms.

27—Northeast light breezes and calms. Extraordinary weather for the place and season. Lat[itude] o[bserved] 31° 14'.

28—Fine southerly winds these 24 hours. 32° 37'.

29—Lat[itude] obs[erved] 35°. Strong wind. Southwest.

30—Very heavy sea. Dirty weather. S. East winds.

31—N.N.E. winds. Fine weather. Sounded 25 fathoms at 4 o'clock; 17 fath[oms] at 6. Tack[e]d. Spoke ship.

FEBRUARY

1—Stood off all night like damned fools and miss the chance of coming in. After 12 [o']clock variable winds and rains.

2—Same fault as day before very far in the morning. N.N.E. winds. Fine cold weather. Saw the land at 11 o'clock. Calms in the morning. Saw Cape He[n]lopen Light House.[1]

3—N.W. winds. Could not get in. Blew very fresh.

4—Same winds. Determined going to New York in sight of Little Egg Harbor.[2] Sailed northwards alo[n]g the co[a]st. Winds O.S.O.[3]

5—Winds northwest. Bitterly cold weather. Saw the High Lands of Navesink.[4]

6—Got a pilot on board early. Calms all day. Saw the light house at 12 o'clock.

---

[1] On the Delaware side of the entrance to Delaware Bay.

[2] Behind Long Beach Island on the New Jersey coast, north of Atlantic City.

[3] The author has fallen into French. Presumably he means W.S.W.

[4] MS *Nevesink*. The coastal ridge between Sandy Hook Bay and the Navesink River estuary, now more commonly called the Atlantic Highlands and the site of a powerful lighthouse.

Appendix

APPENDIX[1]

EXTRAITS DE MON JOURNAL EN ESPAGNE

En sortant de France pour entrer dans la province de
Biscaye vous passez du pays où la liberté a fait le plus de
mal dans celui où elle fait le plus de bien, et ces deux effets
sont également sensibles.

———————

Les Espagnols et les Espagnoles forment deux espèces tout
à fait différentes: les premiers, surtout les Castillans, sont
graves, froids, réfléchis, font tout *poco á poco,* et pincent
même leur guitare avec nonchalance; leurs femmes au con-
traire sont gayes, éveillées, toujours très pressées, et battent
la mesure fort vite.

———————

J'aime beaucoup le costume des dames Espagnoles. La
mantille[2] fait ressortir à merveille ces grands yeux noirs, bien
fendus, bien garnis, et dont on joue si bien, ces belles dents,
cette jolie bouche, un peu grande mais dont la lèvre supéri-
eure est presque toujours couverte d'un vigoureux duvet
qui promet beaucoup et tient encore davantage. Leur jupon
court, noir, orné de franges, de glands, de garnitures est
extrêmement joli. Elles n'ont pas en général la jambe et le
pied très bien, mais aussi les laissent-elles voir sans pré-
tention, sans affectation, comme les françaises qui n'ont

———————

[1]See p. 89, n. 14.   [2]MS *mentille.*

inventé ces longues queues, si sale[s] et si incommodes, que pour avoir un prétexte de se retrousser jusqu'aux genoux lorsqu['] elles sortent à pied.

_____

On assure que les femmes des personnes auxquelles vous êtes recommandées en Espagne vous donnent souvent la vérole, mais en revanche les dînés des maris ne vous donnent jamais d'indigestions.

_____

L'huile d'olive que l'on fait en Espagne [et] avec laquelle on assaison[n]e tout, est un peu moins forte au goût que l'huile de poisson; car on s'y habitue assez facilement mais elle a une odeur âcre et pénétrante qui se propage au loin et qui s'attache à tout. Si vous passez dans la rue au moment où on fait la cuisine, l'odeur du dîné vous prend à la gorge, les muletiers, les mules, leur harnois, tout cela se sent dans la ronde à un quart de lieue sous le vent. Les maisons, les filles d'auberges, les moines, les meubles, tout ce que l'on ne lave pas souvent, et il y a beaucoup de [ces] choses en Espagne, exhale une odeur d'huile qui vous suffoque.

_____

Sur la brune les rues de Madrid sont pleines de deux espèces d'êtres encapuchonnés, les putains et les moines, et vous les prendriez l'un pour l'autre, tant les premières ont l'air modeste et les autres l'air dévergondé.

_____

Les dames espagnoles ont ordinairement un *Cortejo* très jaloux, un mari qui ne l'est pas, et un amant qui les cocufie tous deux.

_____

Il n'y a pas de ville dans le monde où il y ait autant de libraires qu'à Madrid et pas de pays où il y ait autant de livres défendus.

_____

On trouve ici comme dans tous les coins du monde des perruquiers, des modistes, et des maîtres de danse français,

Appendix

mais ce qui est plus extraordinaire est d'y trouver quelques ouvriers anglais qui ont volontairement échangé la liberté, le Roast beef et la porter de la vie[i]lle Angleterre contre l'inquisition, les pigeons étiques, et *l'agua* de la nouvelle Castille.

Environ deux mille personnes vivent à Madrid du produit d'une cruche d'eau qu'ils portent sur l'épaule avec des verres dans un panier pour régaler les passan[t]s. C'est *agua fresca* que l'on vous propose au spectacle au lieu des rafraîchisse-ments[3] ordinaires; aux promenades, dans les rues, c'est toujours *agua fresca*. La maladie qui fait le plus de ravages a Madrid est la colique, et je n'en suis pas étonné.

Quand j'ai parlé de l'odeur de l'huile je n'avais vu que la province; je ne connaissais pas les belles et riches maisons de Madrid. Ici ce n'est point une odeur végétale mais une odeur tout à fait animale qui domine: il y a sous chaque porte une grande auge où le passant peut se satisfaire, où les domestiques vont et vuident de tem[p]s en tem[p]s l'énorme chaise percée qui meuble l'appartement. Le voyage de la chaise percée se sent dans le salon, l'auge parfume les esca-liers et une partie de la maison, et vous êtes toujours dans les palais entre l'or et l'ordure.

Puisque je suis sur le chapitre des odeurs, je ne dois pas oublier celle de l'ail qui est insup[p]ortable au spectacle, à la promenade, dans tous les endroits où il y a beaucoup de monde rassemblé. On pourrait affirmer qu'il est très dif[f]i-cile en Espagne de trouver un petit coin qui ne sente pas l'huile, l'ail, ou la merde.

Il faut voir ce fameux *Prado,* et le prononcer *Prao.* C'est une belle promenade, bien garnie les jours de fête, et qui

---

[3]MS *raffraichissemens.*

ressemble à ce que serai[en]t les grandes allées des Tuileries réunies aux boulevards avec deux files de voitures.

Ces voitures, dont le nombre est surprenant pour une ville comme Madrid, sont ou antiques ou du plus mauvais genre, trainées par les mules atelées avec des cordes, et chargées de domestiques à livrée sale. À Longchamps cette année, nous ne pûmes trouver un seul équipage où il n'y eut pas quelque chose de mauvais goût; au *Prao* il serait aussi difficile d'en trouver une où il y eut quelque chose de bon goût.

Il règne au Prado le plus grand ordre: il y a toujours un détachement de cavaliers entre les voitures, mais à chaque instant la file s'arrête; vous croiriez qu'il est arrivé quelqu'accident; point du tout, c'est qu'une mule a envie de pisser. Cet animal indocile ne tient compte ni du fouet du cocher, ni de la gravité du maître Grand d'Espagne, Évêque, ou chanoine, ni du pudique embarras de la jeune femme qu'elle traîne. Elle écarte les jambes, al[l]onge sa queue pelée [et] se satisfait longuement, et reprend sa marche jusqu'à ce qu'il plaise à une autre d'en faire autant.

Le coup de cloche qui annonce la prière dite *Angelus* fait sur la totalité des promeneurs du Prado le même effet que l'envie de pisser d'une mule sur la file des voitures. Tout est suspendu comme par un [p]ouvoir magique; au bruit le plus confus succède le silence le plus parfait; chacun est arrêté, découvert, recueilli; reste ainsi 5 minutes et ne reprend mouvement et parole que lorsque la cloche aigre et perçante a donné un nouveau signal.

Les rues de Madrid sont assez propres mais le pavé mauvais. Il n'y a qu'une large pierre auprès des maisons sur laquelle on marche à la file et sur laquelle il faut à chaque instant disputer le terrain à ceux qui viennent en sens con-

Appendix

traire. Deux espèces de passan[t]s très communs dans ces rues, les ânes et les prêtres, ne vous cèdent jamais le haut du pavé que vous n'en veniez aux voies de fait.

Les pauvres vous demandent ici l'aumône comme s'il était convenu que ce sont eux qui vous rendent servic[e] en vous procurant cette occasion de gagner le paradis.

Le peuple d'Espagne aime la chasse aux poux[4] comme les princes celle à la grande bête. Ils la font souvent, ils en tuent beaucoup, mais ils seraient bien fâchés d'en détruire l'espèce; ils se priveraient par là d'un passe-tem[p]s, d'un plaisir, d'une occupation.

Rien ne ressemble à nos Indiens d'Amérique comme les Castillans: ils ont la même couleur de peau, les mêmes cheveux, et sont tout comme eux, sales, paresseux, puants, voleurs et fiers, etc., etc.

---

[4]MS *pous*.

Index of Proper Names

INDEX OF PROPER NAMES

Index

Bacciochi, Mme Elisa, 62
Bacciochi, Félix, 62
Badajoz, Peace of, 68
Bahabón, Spain, 67, 91
Baltimore, Md., 97
Banc des Marguerites (Marguerite Bank), France, 118
Bank of the United States, xvii
Baptiste, Capt. (Joseph François Eugène Benjamin, Baron Anselme, called Baptiste), xxi, 9
Barbachano, Ramona María de, 91
see also Adán, Doña
Barbé-Marbois, François, Marquis de, 24, 109, 111
Barbezieux, France, 67, 68, 114
Barcelona, Spain, 67, 88
Barclay, Thomas, 3
Barfleur, Cape, France, 14
Barine, Arvède, *Louis XIV and La Grande Mademoiselle*, 72
Barnet, Isaac Cox, 92–93, 96, 114, 115, 116
Barras, Paul François Nicolas, Comte de, 37
Barrett, Walter *(pseud.)*, *Old Merchants of New York City*, 50
Barthélemy, François, Marquis de, 109–110
Barthélemy Duchesne & Cie (Paris), xix, 8
Barthelemy [and] Duschéne, *see* Barthélemy, Duchesne & Cie
Basque provinces, Spain, 76–77
see also Álava, Biscay, Guipúzcoa
Batavian Republic, xvi, 59
Bauduy (Bauduit), Peter, xxii
Bautru, Guillaume, Comte de Serrant, 99
Bayonne, France, 65–66, 67, 70–71, 76, 92, 93–94
Beauharnais, Vicomte de, *see* Alexandre, Gen.
Beauharnais, Eugène de, 27, 35
Beauharnais, Hortense de, 27
Beauharnais, Josephine de, *see* Bonaparte, Mme
Beauvilliers (restaurant, Paris), 50–51, 99, 100, 101, 103, 104, 105, 106, 107, 108, 109, 110, 112, 113
Bec-d'Ambès, France, 67, 117
Belgium (Belgic), 61

Beliard de Vaubicourt, Louis François, 102
Beliard de Vaubicourt, Marie Antoinette Amélie, *see* Ohsson, Mme d'
Beliard de Vaubicourt, Pierre, 102
Beliard de Vaubicourt, Pierre Jacques Nicolas, 64, 101–102, 107, 110, 111, 112, 113
Beliard de Vaubicourt, Victor, 102
Belliard, *see* Beliard de Vaubicourt
Bénézech, Pierre, 111–112
Benjamin Franklin (ship), xix, xxi–xxii, 3–5, 8–11, 15, 64, 113, 116–120
Bergüenda, Spain, 67, 91
Bernard, Mr., 88
Bernardin de Saint-Pierre, Jacques Henri, 95, 107
Bernier (lawyer, Égreville), 108
Beugnot, Jacques-Claude, Comte, 18, 19–20
Mémoires (ed. Comte Albert Beugnot), 19
Bidart, France, 93
Bidassoa (river, France and Spain), 72
Bidermann, Jacques, xiv, 23–24, 34, 36, 39, 53, 61, 93
Bidermann, James Antoine, 24
Bilbao, Spain, xxi, 67, 89, 90, 91–92
Biles, John A., *Historical Sketches Pertaining to...Asylum*, 66
Biré, Edmond, *The Diary of a Citizen of Paris*, 50
Biscay [Vizcaya] (province, Spain), 76, 90, 123, 127
Archives of the Diputación de Vizcaya, 91
Blandin, Mr., 73, 114
Blandin Frères (Bordeaux), 73, 115
Blaye, France, 67, 97
Blois, France, 67, 99, 113
Boieldieu, François Adrien, 40
Bois-de-Boulogne (Paris), 53, 54
Bois-des-Fossés (residence), France, 23, 108
Bokelman, Mr., *see* Buckelman
Bonaparte, Mme (Marie Josèphe Rose Tascher de la Pagerie [Josephine de Beauharnais]),

Index

Index

Index

Index

Index

Index

Homberg, Grégoire, 17, 50, 60, 106, 107, 111
Homberg, Henry, 17
Honrubia de la Cuesta, Spain, 67, 91
Hôtel de Boston (Paris), 22
Hôtel des Étrangers (Paris), 23
Hôtel de France (Bordeaux), 68
Hôtel de France (Nantes), 98
Hôtel Franklin (Bordeaux), 94, 114, 117
Hôtel de la Marine (Le Havre), 14
Hôtel de Paris (Paris), 25, 42
Hôtel des Sept Frères Maçons (7 Brothers Masons, Bordeaux), 115
Houdar de Lamotte, Charles Antoine, 41, 64, 104
Houdar de Lamotte, Marie Bonne, see Sauvo, Mme
Hubbard, Nicolaas, 112
Humphreys, David, 88, 89, 90, 109–110
Humphreys, Mrs. David (Ann Frances), 87
Humphreys, F. L., *Life and Times of David Humphreys*, 88

Île (Isle) de France (island, Indian Ocean), 117
Île de Ré, France, xii, 35, 67, 98
Imperial University (France), 65
Indre-et-Loire (department, France), 113
Institute, National (France), 16, 25, 35, 65, 103
Interior, Ministry of the (France), 29, 62–63, 112
Invalides, Hôtel des (Paris), 58
Ionian Islands, 65
Iranda, Simon de Arragorry, Marqués de (Marquis d'), 74–75, 88, 90
sister of, 78
Irato, L' (comic opera), 40
Irún, Spain, 67, 72
Irving, Washington, 90
Isle of Pheasants (Île des Faisans, Bidassoa River), 72
Isnard, Mrs., 65

Jacobins, 8, 10, 15, 19, 23, 37, 47, 49, 64

Jameson, John Franklin, *Correspondence* (ed. E. Donnan and F. L. Stock), 106
Jardin des Plantes (Paris), 103
Jardin des Tuileries (Paris), 104
Jay, John, 74
Jay Treaty, 110, 111
Jefferson, Thomas, xii, 41
Johannot, Jean, 25, 62
Jones, Capt. Lloyd (Loid), 5
Jurien, Charles Marie, 46

Kany, Charles E., *Life and Manners in Madrid*, 87
Kean, Mr., 96
Kellerman, Gen. François Christophe de, 111–112, 113
Kellerman, Gen. François Étienne de, 112
Killmaine, Mrs., 99
Kilmaine, Charles Jennings, 99–100
Kin (King, Koenig), Mathias, 9, 11
Koenig, see Kin
Kuscinski, A., *Dictionnaire des conventionnels*, 16

La Chapelle, M., 114, 115
Lacrosse (la Cross), Mme, 106
Lacrosse, Adm. Jean Raymond, Baron de, 106
La Fayette, Mme, 41
La Fayette, George Washington Motier de, 28
La Fayette, Marie Joseph, Marquis de, 28–29, 41, 42, 57
La Force (prison, Paris), xi, 19, 47, 49
Lambert, Mr., 21
Lambert, Mrs. (née Homberg), 20–21
Lamotte, Charles Antoine, see Houdar de Lamotte
Landes (department, France), 69–70
Lang, Mr., 35
Lang Hupet & Gelot (Paris), 35
Langon, France, 67, 94
Lannes (or L'Asne), Gen. Jean, 48
Lansdowne (Landsdown), Marquis of, 55
see also Wycombe, Lord

Index

Index

Mann, M. L., ed., *Yankee Jeffersonian*, 96
Marans, France, 67, 98
Marbois, *see* Barbé-Marbois
Marengo, Battle of, 26
Maret, Hugues Bernard, 34
Marguerite Bank, *see* Banc des Marguerites
María Luisa, Queen of Spain, 88, 90
Maria Theresa, Infanta of Spain, 72
Marine, Ministry of (France), 10, 37, 46–47, 48, 66, 107–108
Mars (ship), 13
Marsollier, Benoît Joseph, 40
Martin, Capt., 117
Martini, Mr., 96, 116
Martinique, West Indies, xv, 26
Mary (ship), 35
Mason, George, 52
Mason, John, 52
Masons, *see* Freemasons
Mazarredo, Francisco, 91
Mazarredo, Adm. José Domingo, 91
Mazuel, 103
Medinaceli (Medina Coeli), Duke of, 81–82
Méhul, Étienne Nicolas, 40
Meillan, Arnaud Jean, 93–94
Mémoires, 94
Méjan, Étienne, 34
Melville, Herman, 51
Melville, Maj. Thomas, Sr., 51
Melville, Maj. Thomas, Jr., 51, 99, 113
Menoir (or Ménoire), Elenoire, *see* Fenwick, Mrs. Joseph
Ménoire, Alexis Guillaume, 65, 98
Merry, Anthony, 106
Messrs. Van Staphorst & Co. (Amsterdam), 112
Messina, Sicily, 104
Mexico, 58
Michel Brothers (of Orléans), 37 *see also* Veuve Michel
Mirambeau, France, 67, 97
Miranda, Spain, 67, 79
Missouri (ship), 3
Missy, de (Demissy ?), 97–98

Moniteur universel, 34, 35, 105, 106, 108, 114
Monroe, James, 39
Mont de Marsan, France, 67, 69
Montansier, Mlle, 42, 53
Montgomery, George Washington, 90
Montgomery, John, 90
Moreau, Gen. Jean Victor, 27
Moreau de Saint-Méry, M. L. E., *Voyage aux États-Unis* (ed. S. L. Mims), 36
Morellet, Abbé André, 35
Morris, Gouverneur, 50
Diary of the French Revolution (ed. B. C. Davenport), 50
Morris, Robert, 50
Morton, John A., 96, 115
Moustier, Élie, Comte de, x, 57
Muller, J. J. (?), 95, 97
Murray, William Vans, 100, 104
Murray, Mrs. William Vans, 101

Nantes, France, 10, 37, 67, 97, 98–99
Napoleon III, Emperor, 27
National Constituent Assembly, xi, 29, 31, 42, 49, 60, 61, 101, 111
National Convention, 16, 17, 25, 33, 93, 101
Naval Records, Office of, *Quasi-War between the U.S. and France*, 38
Navesink (lighthouse, N.J.), 120
Navy, British, x, 13
Navy, French, xiii, xvii, 10, 16, 47
Necker, Anne Louise Germaine, Baronne de Staël-Holstein, *see* Staël, Mme de
Necker, Jacques, 33, 101
Necker (called Necker Germany or Necker de Germany), Louis, 101, 104
Necker (de) Germany, *see* Necker, Louis
Nemours, France, 67, 108–109
Neptune (ship), 3
Nervión (river, Spain), 92
Neuchâtel, Switzerland, 9
Neuville, Mr. La, 115
New Spain, 58

Index

[141]

Index

Index

Index